For my oldest and mo[st]
cherished friend —

Jerry
San Francisco
June 92

INTERPRETATION
AND
INTERACTION

INTERPRETATION
AND
INTERACTION

___
___

Psychoanalysis or Psychotherapy?

Jerome D. Oremland

**with a critical evaluation by
Merton M. Gill**

THE ANALYTIC PRESS

1991   Hillsdale, NJ   London

Published by The Analytic Press, Inc.
365 Broadway, Hillsdale, NJ

Library of Congress Cataloging-in-Publication Data

Oremland, Jerome D.
  Interpretation and interaction : psychoanalysis or psychotherapy?
/ Jerome D. Oremland ; with a critical evaluation by Merton M. Gill.
    p.   cm.
  Includes bibliographical references and indexes.
  ISBN 0-88163-127-2
  1. Psychoanalysis.   2. Psychotherapy.   I. Gill, Merton Max, 1914-
II. Title.
  [DNLM: 1. Psychoanalysis.   2. Psychotherapy.   WM 420 066i]
RC506.074   1991
616.89'17—dc20
DNLM/DLC
for Library of Congress   91-4573
                                                                  CIP

Printed in United States of America
10 9 8 7 6 5 4 3 2 1

Contents

INTERPRETATION
AND
INTERACTION

Preface

It is customary in the preface to a book on psychotherapy to thank one's students, teachers, and patients. After struggling to systematize and formalize these ideas on psychotherapy, I realize that this custom is more than perfunctory, particularly to express the gratitude owed successive generations of students whom I have had in seminars and supervision. The trainees of the San Francisco Mount Zion Psychiatric Clinic, the Psychiatric Services of Children's Hospital of San Francisco, the San Francisco Psychoanalytic Institute, and the San Francisco Institute for Psychoanalytic Psychotherapy and Psychoanalysis, to name but a few who have invited me for panels, conferences, and symposia, have been an invaluable source of fresh ideas. If only these students knew how much I learned from their questions, comments, doubts, and errors. Their penetrating questioning of the morality of our field, and my painful realization that I was often mouthing responses that I knew in my heart were only partially true, strongly motivated this inquiry into the cherished beliefs and practices of psychotherapy.

Special mention must be made of the important contribution to these ideas by a remarkably stable psychotherapy study group of some 15 years' duration that I was privileged to lead. As valuable as the study of the work of inexperienced psychotherapists is, more rewarding and challenging is the discussion of the work of experienced psychotherapists. That the group, which became known as the Hildegard Berliner Study Group, was composed largely of women from the three mental health disciplines—psychiatry, psychology, and social work—vastly added to my knowledge. How enlightening it was for me, a male psychotherapist, to formulate how I would respond to material directed to a woman. How difficult it was to think how I would respond if I were a female psychotherapist. The group, which went on to found the San Francisco Institute for Psychoanalytic Psychotherapy and Psychoanalysis, gave me an unusual opportunity to observe the unique contributions and the limitations of the three lines of education that are the infrastructure of the mental health professions.

Of special importance were teachers, particularly Donald Jackson, Anna Maenchen, and Emanuel Windholz. Although different in personality, style, and orientation, they never failed to honor new ideas and to enter eagerly into discussion. Few teachers were as candid about their work as Don, as tactful and intelligently kind as Anya, and as skillful in understanding of the patient-psychotherapist-supervisor triad as Windy. How fortunate I was to have had them as teachers and as friends as I developed as a psychotherapist, psychoanalyst, and theoretician. By their example they helped me differentiate between skillful teaching and study of clinical material and theory and the pretentiousness and dogmatism that characterize many "teachers" in our field.

My patients contributed much to this project. Often I wince as I consider of what I once thought and did. Unfortunately, there is no protection from future years bringing the same painful response to these ideas. This is the price of working in a dynamic field. I take heart in knowing that my intentions were good.

In reviewing the book, I fear that I underplay the clinical richness of psychoanalysis. I urge the reader to keep in mind that the book is intended to define psychoanalytically oriented psychotherapy, not psychoanalysis. If the contrasts between psychoanalytically oriented psychotherapy and psychoanalysis are not always clear and in fullness favor psychoanalytically oriented psychotherapy, this reflects an assumed greater familiarity with psychoanalysis and exploits the many areas of overlap between the two modalities, a full appreciation of which adds to my thesis that there can be a psychotherapy whose mode of intervention is identical to that of psychoanalysis.

A similar imbalance in presentation exists for the underrepresentation of the details of the process of interactive psychotherapy, even though I offer a number of examples to illustrate the difference between interventions that are analytic and those that are interactive, and I briefly describe an interactive case. Again I remind the reader that the book is to define psychoanalytically oriented psychotherapy, not interactive psychotherapy, a task that would require a volume of its own. Yet, as the reader will discover as the book unfolds, although I recognize the wide and impressive therapeutic capacity of this mode of intervention, I find essential limitations in the results. I must admit that when, despite my best efforts, a psychotherapy moves from psychoanalytically oriented psychotherapy to interactive psychotherapy, I feel it is because I have failed to attain some essential understanding.

I am saddened to reflect on how little of this work became a part of my family's life. Working in isolation is a curse of psychotherapy, an isolation that intensifies as one fully understands the nature of transference and that is only somewhat mitigated by contact with colleagues. It was a great satisfaction when, during a rare discussion of my ideas about the relation of psychoanalytically oriented psychotherapy to psychoanalysis with my daughter, Annalisa, a lawyer, she suggested the image of the double helix.

It is a marked understatement—I am sure welcomed by him—to say that the book benefited immeasurably from Merton Gill's careful readings, important suggestions, and unrelenting search for inconsistencies. I was completely and gratefully surprised when he accepted my offer to write a responding chapter evaluating these ideas. The book was made more readable by my daughter Celia Teter, an editor, and the task much easier by the able assistance of Cynthia Divino, Ph.D. I am particularly appreciative to Paul Stepansky, Ph.D., Editor-in-Chief of The Analytic Press, for recognizing value in the monograph and for making important and specific substantive and stylistic suggestions, and to his staff for their careful expediting of its publication.

Although I am indebted to many generations of psychotherapists and psychoanalytic theoreticians before me, only some of whom found their way into my references, I take sole responsibility for the ideas and the errors as presented.

Jerome D. Oremland, M. D.

CHAPTER 1

Psychotherapy

The concept of mental illness was a mid-18th-century attempt to make mental aberration parallel to physical dysfunction. Viewing mental aberration as parallel to physical illness was a part of the epistemological evolution that, since the Renaissance, had defined a physical, as opposed to a spiritual, world. This liberal humanistic movement, itself derived from many philosophical roots, used a medical model and gave rise to the concepts of mental illness, the mentally ill, the mental patient, and mental treatment. Developing a medical lexicon for mental disturbance was part of the freeing of mental aberration from spiritual connotations. Just as the medical hegemony steadily replaced the religious influence in the study, care, and treatment of physical dysfunction, medical interests replaced the religious influence in the study, care, and treatment of people with mental aberrations. By the early 18th century, physicians were specializing in the mental illnesses. In fact, the first medical "specialist" was the alienist, the forerunner of the modern psychiatrist.

An early systematic attempt to provide rational treatment in this newly defined area of "illness" was the development in the mid-18th century, particularly in the United States, of *moral treatment*. Proceeding on the simple principles of "knowing the patients well and working closely with them," as part of an emerging mental health movement, these proto-mental health professionals, some of whom were physicians, "were confident that the insane could be cured" (McGovern, 1985, p. 10). Moral treatment emphasized the "role of the environment in the cause and treatment of the mentally ill" and advocated "kind treatment to gain the confidence of the patient," regularity in the patient's life, manual labor, constructive activities, and most important, "break[ing] up the 'wrong association of ideas' of the patients and help[ing] them to form 'correct habits of thinking as well as acting' . . . to direct the patients' minds along new and healthy avenues of thought" (pp. 10–12). Essentially a rational kind of psychotherapy was born.

For many reasons, the confusion and lack of clarity about what constitutes psychotherapy continues to exist. The term itself entered the English language in 1901 (*Oxford English Dictionary*) with the founding of the London Psycho-Therapeutic Society. *Psychotherapy* originally was used to describe the psychological prevention and cure of physical disease. The broad hope of the London Psycho-Therapeutic Society reflected the wide interest at the turn of the century in suggestion and hypnosis and in the rudimentary but beginning scientific base for understanding physical disease.[1]

Although the term psychotherapy came into being shortly following the publication in 1900 of Sigmund Freud's *The Interpretation of Dreams,* an association between psychotherapy and psychoanalysis did not flourish until the 1950s. Because psychoanalysis had evolved from hypnosis, understandably the early polemics regarding psychoanalysis as a treatment quickly concerned the distinctions between psychoanalysis and hypnosis (Freud, 1905a, c, 1912, 1916–1917; Ferenczi, 1919, 1923).

Interest in psychotherapy reached an apogee in the 1950s in the United States. This interest arose largely from the desire to expand the therapeutic scope of psychoanalysis, especially with regard to borderlines and schizophrenics, and in response to the theoretical and operational rigidity that progressively characterized psychoanalysis (Fromm-Reichmann, 1950; Sullivan, 1953; Stone, 1954).

---

[1]For our purposes, suggestion and hypnosis are regarded as being on a continuum reflecting degree of formalization. I generally refer to hypnosis rather than suggestion for historical reasons and because of the tendency to see hypnosis as a procedure, just as there is a tendency to regard psychotherapy as procedures. At base, hypnosis is a systematic application of suggestion.

The most important figure in this expansion was Harry Stack Sullivan, an American, who with his colleagues launched the study of interaction (Sullivan, 1953). Sullivan phrased his observations and theories in terms quite different from the closed-system, energic, psychoanalytic formulations epitomized in the metapsychological writings of Heinz Hartmann, Ernst Kris, and Rudolph Loewenstein, which dominated psychoanalytic thought (Hartmann, 1939, 1950; Hartmann, Kris, and Loewenstein, 1946; Kris, 1951). Sullivan's group became known as the Interpersonal School of Psychiatry because of its emphasis on interpersonal processes in development, psychopathology, and psychotherapy.

Although the center of psychoanalytic theory building, training, and practice had shifted from central Europe to the United States after World War II, in an inconsistent way by the early 1950s interpersonal theory had become the theoretical infrastructure of the emerging psychoanalytic psychotherapy, particularly for nonmedical psychotherapists, among whom psychiatric social workers predominated. Traditional psychoanalytic theory continued as the foundation of the increasingly more standardized psychoanalytic procedure, psychoanalysis proper. Psychoanalytic psychotherapy was a particularly American invention.

With the development of ego psychology, spearheaded by Hartmann (1939, 1950), and the expanding recognition of the importance of understanding the development of object relatedness, which came from several sources, particularly Melanie Klein (1932; Klein, Isaacs, and Riviere, 1952; Harry Guntrip (1961), Donald Winnicott (1965, 1971), and W. R. D. Fairbairn (1954), and as psychoanalysis incorporated and systematized an observational base of development (Mahler, 1968; Mahler, Pine, and Bergman, 1975), the dichotomy between interpersonal and psychoanalytic theory began to disappear. This trend toward integration of psychoanalysis as a theory of development, psychopathology, and treatment has somewhat been reversed by Heinz Kohut's (1971, 1977, 1984) self psychology. Although different from interpersonal theory and object relations theory, Kohut attempted to address issues and deficiencies in general psychoanalytic theory similar to the issues that give impetus to interpersonal theory (Oremland, 1985).

With increasing numbers of mental health professionals being trained as psychotherapists in the United States, many of whom received unsystematic, partial, and frequently erroneous psychoanalytic information, the theoretical base for psychoanalytic psychotherapy became a mixture of concepts and descriptions derived from interpersonal theory, object relation views, behaviorial observations, and psychoanalytic developmental formulations. This potpourri of theories and practices applied by the melange of practitioners of highly varying training, especially in the fields of psychiatry and social work, had as its *lingua franca* the developmental, energic, and structural lexicon of psychoanalysis.

This compote of theories and practitioners was matched by the array of people and mental conditions to which it was applied, people ranging from the most regressed, nonverbal, posturing schizophrenics to those suffering the lightest situational disturbances of adolescent or adult life. Psychoanalysis had arrived at its Golden Age. In fact, the Golden Age of psychoanalysis rested more on the widespread application of this melange of theories and styles of practice than it did on psychoanalysis proper. Psychoanalysis, which had successfully freed itself from hypnosis, had a stepchild of unclear dimensions called psychoanalytic psychotherapy, with the psychoanalysts as the theoretical and clinical leaders (Berliner, 1941).

Within the psychotherapeutic enterprise, a rigid hierarchy of disciplines was soon established with institute-trained psychoanalysts, a small and select group of psychiatrists, at the top. Beneath this elite group were the "dynamic" or "psychoanalytic" psychiatrists, who were partially trained in, or at least considered knowledgeable about, psychoanalysis. This larger group of physicians was followed by a much larger group, the social workers, who, abandoning their traditional guidance and case-oriented helping roles, adopted the nonintervening, nondirective, cathartic model that was being touted as psychoanalytic. Operationally, to a large extent the social workers did the clinical work, generally in institutional settings, under the supervision of psychoanalytic psychiatrists, who themselves had been taught, supervised, and treated by the elite psychoanalysts.

Although schematically appealing, such a hierarchical system could not be maintained because of the varying degrees of training and abilities in each of the disciplines. Moreover, the system began to face difficulties because of the dissatisfaction and disillusionment that inevitably came from the nonspecific application of nonspecific theories to overwhelming problems. It is little wonder that the Golden Age of psychoanalysis was to dissolve into the interactive excesses and emphasis on spontaneity, intuition, and absence of training that characterized the "psychotherapeutic" scene in the late 1960s and early 1970s.

Until the 1970s, the role of the psychologist was yet to be strongly felt in the psychotherapeutic community, although within psychoanalysis there was from the beginning a small group of academically trained psychologists with strong clinical interests. These psychologists called basic psychoanalytic formulations into question and asked for systematization and empirical testing of the widely accepted psychoanalytic propositions (Klein, 1973; Schafer, 1964, 1976; Holt, 1965). Aside from this group of academically trained psychologists, clinically trained psychologists, largely because of their exclusion from the psychoanalytic training institutes, gravitated toward the scholastically acceptable and empirically testable learning theories, even though their influence on psychotherapy was minimal. With time, the psychotherapeutic application of learning theory insinuated itself into the hodgepodge of psychotherapeutic techniques as various conditioning techniques. Suggestion was again gaining favor in the psychotherapeutic community. Somewhat bridging both trends, and of singular importance, was Carl Rogers (1942), who developed a highly nondirective technique that gained wide favor because of its easily demonstrable and taught technique.

The most important early attempt within psychoanalysis to bring order to the chaos created by wide and indiscriminate application of psychoanalytic principles to psychotherapy was the American Psychoanalytic Association's 1953 panel, "Psychoanalysis and Dynamic Psychotherapy—Similarities and Differences," reported by Leo Rangell (1954a).

The International Psychoanalytic Association was not to have a major discussion on psychotherapy until 1970 at the Rome meeting at which a panel was presented on "Psychoanalysis and Psychotherapy," chaired by Robert Wallerstein (Adler, 1970). The *Journal of the American Psychoanalytic Association* (Rangell, 1954a), published the panel reports with sections on the Widening Scope of Indications for Psychoanalysis, the Traditional Psychoanalytic Technique and Its Variations, and Psychoanalysis and Dynamic Psychotherapy—Similarities and Differences. Obviously psychoanalysis was searching its boundaries.

The section on Psychoanalysis and Dynamic Psychotherapy—Similarities and Differences (Rangell, 1954a) carried elaborated versions of the 1953 panel presentations by Franz Alexander, Edward Bibring, Freida Fromm-Reichmann, and Rangell and a new paper by Merton Gill, "Psychoanalysis and Exploratory Psychotherapy." In these papers the wide range of terms used to refer to psychoanalytic psychotherapy reflected the groping for a central theoretical structure to organize the thoughts. Rangell (1954b) wrote,

> the experience of the Committee on Evaluation of Psychoanalytic Therapy, set up within the American Psychoanalytic Association in 1947, . . . was never able to pass the initial and vexatious point of trying to arrive at some modicum of agreement to exactly what constitutes psychoanalysis, psychoanalytic psychotherapy, and possibly transitional forms [p. 734].

Gill's (1954) paper was written without his knowing of the 1953 panel and was a response to a variety of publications attempting to define psychotherapy, particularly Alexander's (1927, 1946; Alexander and French, 1946) bold and widely popular departure from psychoanalysis and Fromm-Reichmann's (1950) attempt to place psychotherapy and psychoanalysis on a continuum. Alexander advocated contrived "corrective" interactions by psychotherapists and actively downplayed psychoanalysis as the premier psychotherapy. Fromm-Reichmann saw "free association, recumbency, and similar measures . . . [as not only] not necessary in psychoanalysis . . . but [a] waste [of] time" (p. 795).

Gill's (1954) paper immediately became a classic because of its succinctness, simplicity, and applicability. He began his clarification by pointing out that confusion exists because

> psychotherapy is often discussed without clearly defining whether one is talking about cases in which psychoanalysis would have been theoretically applicable, but could not be used because of external reasons such as a lack of time or money so that psychotherapy with lesser goals is employed, and those in which psychoanalysis is regarded as contraindicated whether because of temporary reasons . . . or more permanent reasons . . .[p. 773].

Of paradigmatic importance was a conceptual advance in which Gill acknowledged that psychotherapy was generic, and psychoanalysis, a subset. According to Gill,

> The word "psychotherapy" is used in two main senses, first as a broad term to include all types of therapy by psychological means, under which psychoanalysis is included, and second in a narrow sense to designate methods of psychological therapy which are not psychoanalysis, even if they are grounded in the theory of psychoanalysis [p. 772].

Gill's paper marked another important advance. Traditionally, psychoanalysis technically was largely defined in terms of differences from suggestion and hypnosis (Freud, 1905a, c; 1916–1917). In Gill's paper, psychotherapy was defined by contrasting it with psychoanalysis. To do so, Gill had to arrive at an operational definition of psychoanalysis, a refinement of Freud's (1916–1917) description of the shibboleth of psychoanalysis, interpretation of resistance and transference. Gill wrote,

> By putting together a number of attempts at definition which have been made, I believe that the essence of the psychoanalytic technique is stated in the following formula: *Psychoanalysis is that technique which, employed by a neutral analyst, results in the development of a regressive transference neurosis and the ultimate resolution of this neurosis by techniques of interpretation alone"* [p. 775].

Psychoanalysis, or at least Gill's definition of psychoanalysis, became the standard against which other psychotherapies were measured and defined.

With regard to the generic concept of psychotherapy, Gill maintained a triadic distinction: supportive psychotherapy, exploratory psychotherapy, and psychoanalysis. Gill differentiated his triad along an axis of *predominate intervention*. Supportive psychotherapy was defined by its predominance of counseling, suggestion, and advice-giving interventions. Exploratory psychotherapy included vaguely defined explorations of causal factors largely in developmental, that is, personal, historical terms. Psychoanalysis was defined by the primacy of interpretation of the transference neurosis. In a general way, supportive and explorative psychotherapies involved lesser frequency of sessions (once or twice a week) and face-to-face positioning; psychoanalysis required greater frequency (three to five times a week) and recumbency of the patient.

To clarify exploratory psychotherapy, Gill introduced a new term, *the intermediate form.* In this expanded concept of what was generally held to be "exploratory," Gill, more than previous writers, blurred the distinctions between psychotherapy and psychoanalysis proper, placing the psychotherapies on a continuum— "primarily supportive or primarily exploratory, with all grades in between" (p. 772). Gill's unclearly formulated "intermediate" form characterized a genre of psychotherapy. Although solving some terminological problems, Gill's proposal raised many theoretical issues. This intermediate form (generally called exploratory psychotherapy) became the overall rubric for the most widely applied form of psychotherapy in America and became synonymous with psychoanalytic psychotherapy (Berliner, 1941). Although Gill (1982) currently and in important ways is assailing his own definition of psychoanalysis and his continuum, his 1954 paper remains a watershed definition of these procedures.

Somewhat later and working within a research framework, Ernst Ticho and Robert Wallerstein (Wallerstein, 1968, 1986), in the now completed Topeka Study, also emphasized the predominance of intervention and differing goals in differentiating the psychotherapies. Following Gill, psychotherapy was seen as the generic enterprise and psychoanalysis as a subset. In the Topeka Study, supportive interventions constituted selective attempts by the psychotherapist to support "healthy" and "nonpathological" defenses through reality testing, selective reinforcements, and role modeling. The goals were modest. Exploratory interventions in the Topeka Study included attempts (unclearly defined) to bring into firmer awareness a variety of events in the patient's life that were regarded as causal of the patient's present difficulties. The treatment goals were broader. Psychoanalysis was seen as the full exploration of the patient's past through the interpretive exploration of transference reenactments with the resolution of the transference neurosis and as carrying the greatest potential for character change. In the Topeka Study's original schema, there was less a sense of continuum between exploratory psychotherapy and psychoanalysis than Gill's paper allowed. In the Topeka Study, as Gill held, frequency of sessions and positioning of the patient reflected the general practice of lesser frequency and face-to-face positioning for supportive and exploratory psychotherapy and greater frequency and recumbency for psychoanalysis.

Because the Topeka Group was researching efficacy and outcome of the psychotherapies, a diagnostic specificity evolved that amounted to a treatment hierarchy. Essentially the research group suggested that most psychotic and some borderline patients benefit, but with limited goals, from supportive psychotherapy and that many would be harmed by "higher level" work. The Topeka Group felt that some psychotics, many borderlines, and most neurotics would benefit from exploratory psychotherapy. Lastly, the Group concluded that some borderlines and most neurotics would benefit from psychoanalysis. With regard to exploratory psychotherapy versus psychoanalysis, the overall implication was that because of broader goals, psychoanalysis was the superior treatment for the suitable patient. Complicated questions concerning the effect of frequency of sessions and the role of the couch were not considered by either Gill or the Topeka Group.

The prestige of the Topeka Group and the general tendency for psychotherapists to seize upon isomorphic correlations that are easily schematized and easily taught resulted in the Topeka terms and the implied therapeutic recommendations being widely accepted long before their follow-up studies were complete. With follow up, many of the original propositions have been significantly modified largely in the direction of seeing less distinction between psychotherapy and psychoanalysis than was originally formulated (Wallerstein, 1986).

THE PSYCHOANALYTIC ORIENTATION

The roots of the psychoanalytic orientation are in Humanism and the early Renaissance. By the late 19th century, rationalism and the optimistic belief in the scientific method, scientism, reached its zenith. Enormous advances in understanding and controlling illness as physical rather than spiritual entities inevitably led to the application of the principles of positivism to the study of psychology and social systems—the birth of the social sciences. Auguste Comte, the founder of sociology, and Wilhelm Wundt, the founder of experimental psychology, were to carry into their respective fields the 19th-century optimistic hope that through understanding, humankind's ancient and modern enemies could be eliminated. Psychoanalysis was to rise directly from this scientific ferment (Sulloway, 1979; Schorske, 1981).

As the social and physical sciences flourished, Freud extended the application of the scientific canon beyond the study of cognitive processes to the exploration of irrational mental processes, the dream, neuroses and the psychoses. In some ways, *The Interpretation of Dreams* (Freud, 1900) is the penultimate application of positivism, evidencing Freud's far-reaching vision and hubris. He was to study the irrational rationally. *The Interpretation of Dreams,* although of clinical importance, primarily is a tour de force in the study of the properties, principles, and laws of mental functioning. Freud's vehicle for studying the irrational was the normal psychosis, the dream. The psychoanalytic orientation is a continuation of the spirit that led to the writing of *The Interpretation of Dreams;* it is primarily investigative. Although easily misconstrued, the psychoanalytic orientation is, in fact, not therapeutic it is investigative—an investigation of the personality.

There are important reasons, epistemological and clinical, to dichotomize the psychoanalytic and the therapeutic orientations. This dichotomy parallels the dichotomy of interpretive interventions, which provide understanding, and interactive therapeutic interventions in psychotherapy. It is important, however, to recognize that *interpretation is interactive and that all aspects of the psychotherapeutic interaction are just that, various kinds of interactions. Yet, interpretation as an intervention is qualitatively different from other interactions in that its aim is solely to add explicit knowledge, whereas interactive interventions remain largely experiential. Most important, when transferential, interpretation makes the interaction itself the object of analysis.*[1] Further, interpre-

---

[1] More precisely considered, interventions are interactive either without analysis of the interaction (interactive interventions) or with analysis of the interaction (interpretive interventions). As Mary Schwartz succinctly put it in discussions with Gill, "interaction with or without interpretation." It was tempting to use her phrase as the title for the book, yet, as accurate as she is, I was concerned that interaction with or without interpretation might be construed as meaning that what is advocated is purposeful interaction with subsequent interpretation, rather

tation, including transferential interpretation, can through selectivity be interactive. As Edward Bibring indicated, "[interpretation] can be employed in a technical sense [to promote the . . . process] or in a curative way [to produce therapeutic changes]" (cited in Rangell, 1954a, p. 160). Recognizing that the tendency to be interactive in psychotherapy is very strong and that interactive interventions can be remarkably palliative raises the question, Why maintain the psychoanalytic orientation? [2]

The psychoanalytic orientation attempts to understand. It does not offer the promise of relief, healing, or cure (medical concepts) or salvation (a religious concept). The psychoanalytic orientation offers knowledge, not amelioration. It is an educative approach, an "after-education" as Freud (1917) called it.[3]

The interactive (therapeutic) orientation compromises knowledge for remission and is congruent with Leo Stone's (1961) understanding of the physicianly role of the psychoanalyst and the patient's expectations of the physician. Sandor Ferenczi (1912), in his untactful but penetratingly insightful way, said, "Suggestion [interaction] artificially encourages the narrowing of consciousness and . . . is an education in blindness" (p. 57).[4] Interactive work carries the message: Do not look; what you see will hurt you. The psychoanalytic orientation carries the message: It is better to see,

---

than considering interpretation as a special kind of interaction that provides explicit verbalized scrutiny of the on-going interactivity that constitutes any psychotherapy. In fact the book might well have been titled *Interaction With or Without Interpretation: Psychoanalysis or Psychotherapy.*

[2]The evaluation of palliation is exceeding complex, for it must take into account, among many things, short-term versus long-term effects, breadth and depth of change, and the more rarely discussed, at what cost to the personality.

[3]James Strachey (Freud, 1916–1917) noted that the German word *Nacherzeihung* is often wrongly translated as "reeducation" rather than "'after-education." What I have in mind are new perspectives gained through reliving and emotional-cognitive reevaluation, a vitalized insight. More precisely, the effect is a meta-education.

[4]Ferenczi was the innovator and past master of nearly all ethical (and some unethical) interactive techniques that are used today, techniques that he called "active techniques" (Ferenczi, 1920, 1925). His term carries the unfortunate connotation that psychoanalytic techniques are passive. Ferenczi's work would have benefited had he differentiated kinds of activity, that is, interpretive versus interactive interventions.

that is, to know. That it is better to know is the singular value of the psychoanalytic orientation.

The metaphors of blindness and seeing are apt because of the close association between the psychoanalytic orientation and insight. The interactive versus the analytic dimension can be considered along an experiential versus insightful axis as long as experiential is narrowly defined as related to those interactions that incorporate experience, and insightful is expanded to include emotive understanding.

In asserting the primacy of knowledge, the psychoanalytic orientation follows the tradition of such courageous explorers as Copernicus. Copernicus dared to proclaim that it is better for humankind to know fully its insignificance in the greater cosmos than to maintain a palliating feeling of being the center of it. Copernicus personifies the psychoanalytic orientation and its singular value: It is better to know.

It is not accidental that Freud (1917, 1925) likened his task to that of Copernicus and of the later, equally iconoclastic Charles Darwin. Freud's concept of the unconscious, like Copernicus's debunking of the central place of the human being in the cosmos and Darwin's debunking of the uniqueness of the development of the human being, poses threats of incredible magnitude to humankind's narcissism. Paradoxically, Copernicus, Darwin, and Freud all unveiled humankind's narcissistic—and other—vulnerabilities and our defenses against them while simultaneously proclaiming the extraordinary power of the uniquely human attribute, rationality. In effect, Copernicus through reason conceived the cosmos; Darwin through reason arrived at the true distinction between humankind and animals; and Freud through reason made conscious the unconscious.

Freud's "aftereducation" is an exact term. Aftereducation captures the sense of layering that characterizes the psychoanalytic view of personality. Psychoanalytically, personality is composed of accretions, changing continuances, and new additions. There is at once flux and continuities. The idea of transformations and accretions in the personality was epitomized by James Joyce (1986) when Stephen Dedalus in *Ulysses* referred to the "I, I and I"(p. 154).

Psychoanalytically, change consists of modifications with continuances. Change in psychoanalysis is not simply the result of education; it is the result of integrating new explanations and new understanding. Such an educative, insight-adding effect is not to be confused with an affect-sparse, life-distant intellectualization or instructive catechism.

Just as the 19th-century appliers of positivism to physical, medical, and social problems optimistically thought that through reason all things would be made better, the psychoanalytic orientation—not in the therapeutic, but in the social science, tradition—carries the promise of potential improvement in that the more one knows, the broader one's choices can be. This is the essence of psychoanalytic orientation: to allow for the development of the greatest repertoire of enlightened choices. It is a mode, not the content.

It is in the limitations of palliation that powerful criticism of interactive psychotherapy can be made. Interactive psychotherapy is largely based on endowment of attributes—selected transferences (externalizations) that are subsequently internalized and to varying degrees integrated. The effects of interactive psychotherapy are relatively limited by the range and scope of the internalizations. What develops is relatively fixed by actual and imagined aspects of the psychotherapist, more accurately by selected, idealized externalizations and reinternalizations by the patient.[5]

In contrast, the psychoanalytic orientation attempts to transcend the idealizations, externalizations, and internalizations by making the motivations for these processes the object of study. In essence, the psychoanalytic orientation is one of knowing, of learning about what the person does with others, which, in turn, translates into a potential "therapeutic." The more one understands about what one is attempting to do, in the broadest sense, with another, the more one will, in the best sense, know oneself.

The recognition of the epistemological significance of the dichotomy between the psychoanalytic and the therapeutic orientation, was early made by Philip Rieff (1968) in *The Triumph of the Therapeutic*. In this slender and prophetic book, Rieff contrasted

---

[5]In brilliant anticipation of our present knowledge about the role of externalization and reinternalization in personality development, Ferenczi (1913b) hypothesized such a sequence of externalization and reinternalization in understanding the development of the sense of reality. His concept might have reached broader currency in psychoanalytic theory had he a clearer concept of object relatedness, its development, and its relation to the interpersonal aspect of sense of reality.

Sigmund Freud and Carl Jung, Wilhelm Reich (his later work), and David Herbert Lawrence as personifications of the dichotomy. Rieff contrasted Freud's psychoanalytic orientation with the remissive therapeutic requirements (that there be a therapeutic result) responded to by the other three.

The most prominent and influential of Freud's early associates, extenders, deviators, and critics that Rieff studied was Carl Jung. Jung was the son and grandson of fundamentalist Christian pastors. His father suffered from psychosis, and in his autobiography, *Memories, Dreams, Reflections,* Jung (1963) admitted to his own lifelong struggle with psychosis. Jung was the most important, creative, and enduring of the three men selected by Rieff to contrast with Freud. Of the many threads running through Jung's ideas, Rieff emphasized the compatibility of Jung's views and Christian mysticism. Rieff (1968) noted that some sectors of organized Christianity were to find in Jung a new leadership: "The religious feelings needed a psychological renaissance less traditionally Christian and yet broad enough to permit a fresh Christian apologetic to be read into it" (p. 42). As a complement, "Jung could not avoid finding a theology at the end of his therapy . . ." (p. 29).

Pointing to Jung's ameliorating tendencies, Rieff said,

> To cure, in the Jungian theory, is to give the patient peace in adhering to the eternal order, replicated within him symbolically [pp. 88–89]. Perhaps, the freedom to choose is not therapeutic enough . . . the content of the choice itself must be recommended, if not prescribed . . . [p. 90]. The Jungian mode of psychoanalyzing was [to quote Jung] "a new message of salvation" . . . [p. 91].

Jung's peace in adherence to the eternal order is in marked contrast to Freud's pursuit of knowledge for its own sake. As Rieff noted, "Being analytic rather than remissive, the Freudian doctrine was never to be put in systemic service to either interdiction or release, under pain of ceasing to be analytic" (p. 238).

As seemingly different from Jung as the radical, flamboyant, disorganized, and tragic Wilhelm Reich was, the two met in religious zeal:

> Furthest to the left of Freud, balancing Jung on the right, was Wilhelm Reich [p. 141]. "Reich started on the left, but kept going, until he found himself

advocating a most radical rejection of politics—a rejection so radical that it must be called religious [p. 142].

Reich, an early associate of, and older than, Freud, was quickly recognized as brilliantly intuitive and therapeutically able; yet, the analytic attitude was never integral to his approach.[6] His work soon became dominated by his view of the therapeutic importance of liberation of the instincts and energies, reifyingly conceived.

[Reich] found himself the center of a therapeutic sect . . . he had passed beyond the analytic attitude to a polemical one. He had become in fact, a Freudo-Marxist [pp. 142–143].

There is a sinister anti-intellectualism about Reich's theory of the origin of repression. Repression began the moment man made the mistake of thinking about himself. . . Reich believed that our sickness began at the moment man began to think—too much and specifically about himself [p. 153].

Early on, Reich aimed at using psychoanalysis for social revolutionary, that is, social therapeutic, purposes. Reich was to go beyond the treatment of the individual as he envisioned the overthrow of the state, a power that Reich, with distorted genius, knew rested with the family, the core oppressive instrument of society. Always quick to apply his ideas, Reich called for radical (therapeutic) revision of society based on the overthrow of the family. He wrote, "It is the authoritarian family that represents the foremost and most essential source of reproduction of every kind of reactionary thinking; it is a factory where reactionary ideology and reactionary structures are produced" (Reich, 1947, p. 60). According to Rieff (1968), "To destroy the ideology and social structure without destroying the factory in which they were manufactured seemed [to Reich] an obvious folly" (p. 156).

Reich's views of nature and his call for movements of radical

---

[6]Reich had his greatest success and his tragic end in the United States. Generally, psychotherapeutic modalities including psychoanalysis as psychotherapy have had their greatest popularity in the United States. It probably is true that the American therapeutic industry conceived of by Rieff (and Freud) as an outgrowth of the excessive medical influence on psychoanalysis has moved psychoanalysis in an ameliorative direction. "Americans, in particular, have managed to use the Freudian doctrine in ways more remissive than he intended . . ." (Rieff, 1968, p. 238).

change proclaimed a power derived from liberating an increasingly reified sexual energy.

> It was his passion to recapture what he considered was the organic sense of wholeness characteristic of the primitive, as against the mechanistic sense of fragmentation he considered characteristic of the modern and scientific world view [Rieff, 1968, p. 179].

As Reich's therapeutic views grew more elaborate, he, in his idealization of things natural, called for sexual play and sexual freedom beginning at birth, a theme not again so overtly proclaimed until the flower children of the 1960s. For Reich, as for many subsequent social reformers, the child was the instrument for social change, and he envisioned a children's crusade against authority. He coupled the idealization of nature and the idealization of children with an idealization of "the worker."

Inevitably Reich "gave up trying to understand altogether. . . . [He] offer[ed] the ecstatic attitude as superior to the analytic" (Rieff, 1968, p. 188). "In this religious doctrine, fear of self not disobedience of God is the original sin" (p. 152). In some ways the single-mindedness of Reich's views, with its intense purposefulness, typifies the narrowness that often accompanies the therapeutic attitude. In present day American psychotherapy, this attitude often manifests itself as variations of liberal, middle-class values. Reich's call for freedom, like that of the interactive psychotherapist, becomes a call to be like the leader.

Less important as a theoretician and never a practitioner, the English novelist D. H. Lawrence, an important early critic of psychoanalysis, was to "inveigh against all abstractions, including psychological ones. The original sin against life is abstract thought" (Rieff, 1968, p. 194). "[S]uch approaches intellectualize the genuinely erotic out of life . . ." (p. 227). To Lawrence, the self was the center of the universe.[7]

Of paramount importance, Lawrence saw commitment as the therapeutic goal. Accurately sensing that to the extent psychoanalysis is analytic it cannot become communal, Lawrence decried

---

[7]This idea may be less in contradiction to those of Copernicus than it seems on first reading. Although modern physics has made it abundantly clear that humankind is not at the center of the universe, the self may be in the sense that the self is a perceiving, rather than a physical, entity.

psychoanalysis and the psychoanalytic movement because it had no potential as a theory of commitment.

The various responses to Freud that Rieff detailed can be seen as attempts to provide, to use Rieff's propitious phrase, "the contents of choices" beyond analysis (p. 90). Jung, Reich, and Lawrence, through their words and actions, decried that Freud stopped short. In response, they proclaimed doctrines. Jung (1963) inadvertently and definitely unintentionally, I feel, paid Freud the ultimate compliment when he stated in his stinging paper "Sigmund Freud in His Historical Setting" that Freud's theory did not stand for a new way of life. I think there are all too many unfortunate examples of what happens when psychoanalytic theory or, worse yet, psychotherapy becomes a way of life.

Similarly limiting, interactive psychotherapy, with its selective internalizations of new objects—objects that paradoxically largely, but not solely, resided split off and negated within the patient—heavily relies on the psychotherapist as template (Bibring, 1937; Stone, 1954; Eissler, 1958; English, 1965; Langs, 1982; Roth, 1987). The psychotherapy, however palliative, creates within the patient versions of the psychotherapist (Oremland, 1972).

The therapeutic contamination of the psychoanalytic orientation personified by Reiff as Jung, Reich, and Lawrence can be seen even in the most carefully conducted psychoanalytically oriented psychotherapy and psychoanalysis (Oremland, Blacker, and Norman, 1975; Norman et al., 1976). Those who have completed such work feel enriched by an appreciation of, and to a degree a submission to, a higher order of organization (Jung); they have the sense of having joined a movement with a new view of how humankind can be (Reich); and often they have a sense of new commitment and, paradoxically, through that commitment freedom (Lawrence). As in all psychotherapy, what is important is predominance. The crucial question determining if the psychotherapy is psychoanalytic or psychotherapeutic is whether its predominant effect comes from such contaminations or is derived from an appreciation of the power (and the limitations) of rational understanding. This book focuses on the distinction between psychoanalytically oriented and interactive interventions in psychotherapy.

CHAPTER 2

Psychoanalytically Oriented Psychotherapy

With the great increase in interest in psychoanalysis following World War II, there evolved a variety of terms to describe the widening range of procedures within the psychotherapy enterprise. Generally the psychoanalytic psychotherapies, regardless of the practitioner or the "patient," were held as distinct from guidance and case work (even when psychoanalytically informed); and from psychoanalysis, which generally was operationally defined, that is, requiring sessions four to five times a week, use of the couch, instruction in free association, and a practitioner fully trained as a psychoanalyst. To emphasize the tie to psychoanalysis and the prestige that psychoanalysis enjoyed, such terms as psychoanalytic psychotherapy, psychoanalytically oriented psychotherapy, and psychoanalytically informed psychotherapy were devised. The terms were used interchangeably to label the *affinity* of the psychotherapist to psychoanalysis as a theory, as an institution, and as a subculture. The common bond was that the psychotherapist loosely used a variety of versions of psychoanalytic constructs to understand the patient, the therapeutic interaction, and to guide the interventions.

Distinguishing the psychoanalytic psychotherapies by the fact that the psychotherapeutic interaction is understood psychoanalytically is not sufficient, for all interpersonal interaction can be understood psychoanalytically. Thus, the question is raised: Is there a subset within the psychoanalytic psychotherapies that is, in essentials, technically as well as theoretically identical to psychoanalysis?[1] I answer yes and suggest redefining the term *psychoanalytically oriented psychotherapy* for this form of psychotherapy.

The term psychoanalytically oriented psychotherapy generally is regarded as having been coined by Frieda Fromm-Reichmann to describe her application of psychoanalytic theory to the treatment of severely regressed schizophrenics. Fromm-Reichmann (1950) wrote, "From this formulation of 'intensive psychotherapy' my psychiatric philosophy becomes evident: there is no valid *intensive* psychotherapy other than that which is psychoanalytic or psychoanalytically oriented" (p. 2).

The use of various psychotherapeutic techniques while maintaining a psychoanalytic understanding of the patient and the process has historical precedent. In his widely quoted introduction to August Aichhorn's *Wayward Youth,* Freud (1925) noted,

> The possibility of analytic influence rests upon quite definite preconditions which can be summed up under the term "analytic situation"; it requires the development of certain psychical structures and a particular attitude to the analyst. Where these are lacking . . . something other than analysis must be employed, though something which will be at one with analysis in its *purpose* [p. 100].

Fromm-Reichman evolved her psychoanalytically oriented psychotherapy technique from an interpersonal psychoanalytic theoretical framework and the disturbed patients whom she was treating. Even though what she had in mind technically is quite different from what I propose, the linguistically awkward term psychoanalytically oriented psychotherapy carries the promise of a precision of definition that eliminates some of the confusion regarding the psychotherapies.

I favor the term psychoanalytically oriented psychotherapy be-

---

[1]"Technically identical" refers to the technical essentials. The technical essential of psychoanalytically oriented psychotherapy, like psychoanalysis, is that the predominant intervention is interpretation of the transference. In that way, what the psychotherapist does in psychoanalytically oriented psychotherapist and the psychoanalyst does in psychoanalysis are "technically identical"; how the patient responds may be different owing to several factors, including case selection, recumbency, and greater frequency of sessions in psychoanalysis.

cause I want to emphasize the *orientation of the psychotherapy* as opposed to the *orientation of the psychotherapist*. The shift to delineating the orientation of the psychotherapy rather than the orientation of the psychotherapist has the advantage of allowing differentiations to be based on an evaluation of the psychotherapeutic interventions, an approach similar to Gill's (1954) and later the Topeka Group, but an approach not carried far enough by either.

The psychotherapies, including psychoanalysis, have much in common, including a variety of noninterpersonal, as well as interpersonal, effects. Noninterpersonal experience, such as the sense of mastery and control of the diffuse and the subjective, characteristically comes with putting ideas and feelings into words. Subtle changes in perspective and a subjective sense of "catharsis" come with retelling an incident that is mildly or severely disturbing.[2] Abreaction, the recalling of forgotten traumatic memories, is a therapeutic component of all psychotherapies, although generally overrated.

Among the more overtly interpersonal aspects of the psychotherapeutic experience is the feeling of being understood, often spurious, in a nonjudgmental atmosphere. More complex, the role of confession-absolution and self-forgiveness as personal revelations are made to an apparently accepting, knowing, wise other has strong ontological and historical precedent. The skillful use of questions, clarifying comments, and subtle suggestions and inferring good and bad consequences can profoundly change a person's direction and mode of living. Anyone who studies the process material of all the psychotherapies, including psychoanalysis, is struck by the enormity of the role of specific and nonspecific suggestive interpersonal interaction (Roth, 1987; Wallerstein, 1986).

Although a division can be made between specific and nonspecific suggestive interpersonal aspects, the superordinate consideration regarding the nature of the psychotherapy is the identification

---

[2]The idea of alleviation of anxiety through "discharge" of affect, catharsis, is misleading. It probably stems from early overuse and reification of energic metaphors in psychoanalytic theory. On close scrutiny, even such an apparently noninterpersonal expressive experience as a barely verbalized expletive, a mumbling to oneself, to the more formalized writing of a diary is psychodynamically a "conversation" with another, an appeal to the primal other.

of that aspect of the interaction that relies on the patient's endowing the psychotherapist and the psychotherapy with complex constructs—the highly varied potential for intense projection and multifaceted interpersonal fantasies.[3] It is in this dimension of psychotherapy—the patient's endowing the psychotherapist and the psychotherapy with intense, multifaceted emotive contents— that the regressive potential inherent in interpersonal interaction, specifically the transference, resides.

Interactive versus Psychoanalytic Interventions: A New Triad

Thus far I have described various interactive psychotherapeutic potentials common to all the psychotherapies that may be intensified to bring about specific behavioral and more general personality modification. Missing in the discussion is distinguishing interactive interventions from psychoanalytic interventions, a consideration that returns us to Gill's (1954) operational definition of psychoanalysis as a psychotherapeutic process with resolution of the transference through interpretation.

I suggest that among the psychotherapies guided by psychoanalytic theory can be a psychotherapy in orientation identical to psychoanalysis. As in psychoanalysis, the orientation in this psychotherapy is toward full interpretation of the transference while maintaining the face-to-face positioning and the lesser frequency (two times a week) of sessions. Such a differentiation maintains a triad for the psychoanalytically informed psychotherapies but requires different terms reflecting the different emphasis.

To emphasize the orientation of the psychotherapy (rather than the orientation of the psychotherapist), I replace *exploratory psycho-*

---

[3]Freud's term *Bezetzung* (occupation, filling) was translated by James Strachey (1962) to *cathexsis,* a word he coined from the Greek *catechein* (to occupy). Although originally devised to describe the concentration on and transfer of psychic energy to a person, idea, or thing, cathexsis is of broader value when considered in contextual rather than energic terms. Cathexsis can best be considered as an investing with or endowing of a process, an idea, or an other with emotive ideational contents.

therapy with *psychoanalytically oriented psychotherapy* to indicate a psychotherapy identical in orientation to psychoanalysis—the exploration of the personality through understanding and interpretation of the transference.

Also from this view, *supportive* psychotherapy is overly inclusive and does not accommodate to the fact that the most supportive intervention is accurate interpretation. To emphasize that in so-called supportive psychotherapy the interventions are generally unanalyzed interactions, I propose that psychotherapies that emphasize interactive intervention be called interactive psychotherapy. Rather than the widely used triad—supportive psychotherapy, exploratory psychotherapy, and psychoanalysis—my triad of the psychoanalytically informed psychotherapies becomes *interactive psychotherapy, psychoanalytically oriented psychotherapy,* and *psychoanalysis.*

Although it is tempting to call the interactive member of my triad psychoanalytically interactive psychotherapy, the term carries a different referent and is not parallel to the term psychoanalytically oriented psychotherapy. Psychoanalytically interactive psychotherapy refers to the psychotherapist and connotes that the psychotherapist uses a psychoanalytic view of psychopathology and personality development, that the psychotherapist is psychoanalytically oriented. Psychoanalytically oriented psychotherapy refers to the psychotherapy and connotes that the psychotherapy is psychoanalytically oriented. From this point of view, an interactive psychotherapist can be psychoanalytically oriented or not; for example, the psychotherapist can be religiously oriented. Generally when referring to interactive psychotherapy, I have in mind that the psychotherapist is fully trained in psychoanalytic theory; that is, the psychotherapist is psychoanalytically oriented but *chooses* to use interactive rather than interpretive interventions.

To place the psychoanalytic orientation in bold relief, I present, by way of contrast to psychoanalytically oriented psychotherapy, a psychotherapeutic interactive interchange. (see Oremland, 1976):

A 28-year-old unmarried female explained on the telephone that she had been having difficulties with "swelling of her tongue." As the swelling became more severe she contacted her internist, who, recognizing the psychological component, suggested that she contact a psychiatrist. She mentioned on the telephone that she was leaving for Europe in the early part of the following week and asked if I could see her soon.

A tall, strikingly handsome young woman, she carried herself with unusual grace and dressed with striking beauty. She was a painter and had recently been invited to join a woman friend, also a painter, in Europe. The friend had written that it was a "perfect time—the museums are uncrowded and we can visit artist friends and the various academies where we know people."

The patient explained that she had not been to Europe for some eight years, although she knew it very well. Her mother and father, both renowned artists, had sent her to private school in Switzerland when she was young to study art, master French, and become "culturally" educated. On completing school, she had continued studying art in Switzerland and became an ardent skier, skillful enough for her to become a ski instructor. Her friends were mostly ski instructors from all over Europe, and she vividly described a "dashing life." She noted that her skiing had became "more and more aggressive" as she become more interested in racing with male skiers. Once while racing, she had suffered a bad fall and severely fractured her leg, necessitating surgery. She had hobbled home in a large cast.

On returning home she had enrolled in the local art institute and quickly became involved with the teacher, a highly esteemed artist some 30 years older than she. During the ensuing years, she devoted less time to her painting and more time to caring for him. In the past several years there had been a growing dissatisfaction between them, each recognizing that she was hiding herself in the relationship. Recently she had become annoyed by evidences of his being older and his "exaggerating his infirmities." A precipitating incident occurred approximately three months before she came to see me, when he asked her to adjust the shawl on his shoulders. With annoyance she accused him of pretending that he was Renoir, the crippled master. They separated amicably about a month later.

Shortly thereafter her friend in Europe encouraged her to visit. It was at the airline office that she noted a peculiar difficulty in talking, that her tongue seemed to become "thick and stiff" and her lips "to swell" as she tried to get information about flights. After that, whenever she talked about "the trip," her tongue would swell. At first she thought it was a peculiar allergy that caused her "tongue and lips to swell." While she was talking with me in the office, as she said "the trip," her mouth puckered up and her words became indistinct. She seemed to be struggling helplessly, at the same time bemused, as her speech became indistinct. Several times during the session, she said in a most distorted way, "See, there it's happening right now!" and pointed to her mouth.

As the interview developed and her symptoms were clarified, I told her that I felt that the symptom represented her fear of speaking for herself. I told her that for many years, apparently, she could allow herself to develop only vicariously. I indicated that she had helped her artist boyfriend do what she could not allow herself to do—develop, assert, and achieve. I suggested that the skiing accident had frightened her, that perhaps it had seemed a "deserved" punishment for being competent and assertive and that subsequently she was fearful of such strivings.

She was interested in what I had to say and then asked me directly if she should proceed with the trip. She indicated that she could delay it and continue seeing me if I thought it necessary. I indicated that, though she could continue to see me, she could take the trip and could easily return if her difficulties continued. As she left, she said that she felt more "secure" and if she had continuing difficulty she would call me and perhaps return for further consultation.

My next contact with her was some three months later, when I received a postcard from Amsterdam. The picture on the postcard, Rembrandt's *Self-portrait, open-mouthed* with his lips pursed, bore a striking resemblance to her expression when she had talked about "the trip" (see Figure 1).

The message on the postcard read,

Dear Dr. Oremland, My friend and I are enjoying the museums and galleries. I have had no further difficulties and am glad that I decided to make the trip.

I very much appreciated your help and will call you when I return if it is necessary. Sincerely, [signed].

About eight months later I chanced to see her at an art gallery opening. I approached her and asked if she remembered me. She said, "Why, of course, Dr. Oremland, I am very grateful to you. I

Figure 1. *Self-portrait, open-mouthed,* 1630. Etching, only state, 51 × 46 mm. Bottom centre: RHL 1630. Reproduced with the kind permission of Museum het Rembrandthuis, Amsterdam.

have several times thought to call, but there has really been no reason." She went on to describe how well she was doing, how significantly her art was developing, and how proud she was that an exhibition of her work was soon to open.

I asked if she recalled the postcard. She said, "Yes, I think it was from Amsterdam" but offered little more. There was a pause. She looked a little quizzical and asked, "Was there something about it?" I said, "It was beautiful. Do you remember the picture!" She answered, "No. Well, yes, I believe it was a Rembrandt etching." She then talked about her long-standing interest in his etchings. She laughed and said, "I do love those Rembrandt etchings don't you? They say so much."[4]

---

[4]In the 1976 essay, I speculated on the relation of the etching to her hysterical symptom and possible ways its selection further resolved her conflict.

She went on to describe the developments in her painting, "My work is becoming much bolder and firmer," and mentioned a recent interest in male nudes. We exchanged some pleasantries and parted.

Even though specific developmental linkages cannot be made for lack of historical details, it was relatively easy to come to a dynamic understanding of this young woman's acute symptom. The skiing injury became a symbolic punishment for assertive, exhibitionistic, competitive success with men. The injury resulted in her inhibiting and defending against phallic strivings by devoting herself to an older, already accomplished man. Vicariously she participated in his achievement without having to continue her own. With his "failing" she could no longer use him to cover her phallic strivings, and they amicably decided to part.

She was offered the opportunity of experiences in Europe to resume an active life. Ironically, her first step away from her eight-year bondage was unconsciously related to the precipitating circumstances of that bondage.

The assertive, aggressive potential of her tongue became the central focus of displaced castration concerns. Her tongue seemed "to swell and stiffen," inhibiting her speech. As the symbolic representation of assertive, competitive, exhibitionistic strivings, it became the wished for and feared erection. At the same time, its inflexibility rendered it impotent. In a sense, like the cast on her leg, it became the erect phallus, a power that also cripples. The "swelling tongue," with its interference with speech, became in the classical hysterical sense a compromise formation symbolizing the phallic wishes and the punishment for them. Though at one level distressing, at another level it provided *primary* gain evidenced by the "belle indifference" typical when conflict is resolved in specific hysterical symptoms.

My *selective interpretation of the psychodynamics* enabled her to gain insight into the meaning of the symptom. I indicated that the symptom protected her from asserting herself, just as the relationship with the older man had. By encouraging her to continue with her plans, I at once endorsed her asserting herself and discouraged her from involving herself, potentially endlessly, once again with an older man (me).

During my chance meeting with her eight months later I was able to confirm that there had been no return of the symptom and that she was actively and efficiently painting. When I pressed for details about the etching, she became mildly annoyed and gave no indication that she had consciously selected that particular postcard. In her response, "The etchings say so much," the metaphoric use of *say* may have revealed a derivative representation of the central symptom, inhibited speech, and the power of my interpretation many months before.

From a therapeutic standpoint, my selective interpretation appears to have "loosened her tongue" and allowed her to "speak for herself." That interpretation, coupled with my encouraging her to continue with her plans—in effect, my encouraging her to face the "danger"—moved her in a direction. By reminding her that she could return, I provided a protection. I was available and could help if necessary. I was fully on the side of mastering assertion conflicts *using* the transference and selective insight toward that specific goal,[5] that is, insight that is selected by the psychotherapist but that is necessarily partial and incomplete.

Most important, I actively inhibited her invitation to establish again a prolonged, perhaps, serving relationship with an older man. Yet, at the same time, she was deprived of the opportunity of reexperiencing with full genetic exploration and understanding the unresolved infantile conflicts that had given form to her characterological tendencies, determined the response to her skiing accident, *and* underlay *the* symptom. Thus, this interactive encounter, although therapeutically helpful, in effect deprived her of the optimal opportunity to alter moderately severe characterological tendencies that, left unattended, continue silently, perhaps interfering with her full living.[6]

---

[5]Although the situation was seen as an acute problem best handled by an interactive attempt to help the patient achieve mastery by setting in motion continuing, previously aborted development, the therapeutic approach also reflected unrecognized countertransference responses—I, for whatever unconscious reasons, was reluctant to involve her in what she had only recently freed herself from. Successive generations of students seemingly take delight in asking whether my "insightfulness" might have been a seductive interaction and whether, because she was so attractive, I "sent her on her way" out of countertransference anxiety.

[6]Although the illustration demonstrates how selective interpretation and the transference can be used toward therapeutic goals, I fear that it overemphasizes a dramatic and brief psychotherapy. In practice, most interactive work is prolonged,

In *interactive psychotherapy* specific interpersonal aspects of psychotherapy are consciously intensified to achieve specific treatment goals; that is, the psychotherapist conscientiously uses a large variety of interventions, including interpretations, as overt and covert directives and suggestions. In *psychoanalytically oriented psychotherapy*, as in psychoanalysis, as will be developed later, specific interactive aspects are consciously minimized and, to the fullest extent possible, are identified as being components and concomitants of the transference. As these manifestations are identified as components of the transference, they are interpreted in the current dynamic context and, to the extent possible, in genetic developmental terms. The transference is not *used* for psychotherapeutic aims; it is *interpreted*.

As previous noted, interactive psychotherapy, psychoanalytically oriented psychotherapy, and psychoanalysis have strong, nonspecific interpersonal aspects that move the patient in certain directions. Yet in psychoanalytically oriented psychotherapy and in psychoanalysis these nonspecific interpersonal aspects are intentionally minimized, whereas in interactive psychotherapy they are ignored or even maximized (Wallerstein, 1986).

This distinction between interventions in interactive psychotherapy and psychoanalytically oriented psychotherapy was approached by Ralph Greenson (1967) when he stated,

> Every definition of psychoanalytic technique must include as a central element the *analysis* of transference. Every deviant school of psychoanalysis can be described by some aberration in the way the transference situation is handled. Transference reactions occur in all patients undergoing psychotherapy. Psychoanalysis is distinguished from all other therapies by the way it . . . attempts systematically to analyze transference phenomena [p. 151].

The difference between *using* and *interpreting* the transference, in essence, is the principle that differentiates interactive work from psychoanalytic work and that marks the orientation of psychoanalytically oriented psychotherapy and psychoanalysis as identical. It is worth restating that interpretation is a form of activity qualitatively different from other interactive interventions in that its aim

----

and the suggestive-directive aspects are highly subtle and complex. Most often, the psychotherapist has little awareness of the full significance of the interventions.

primarily is to add knowledge; and when the interpretation is transferential, the interaction itself becomes the object of the analysis. The differences between psychoanalytically oriented psychotherapy and psychoanalysis, differences that tend to be minimized in Gill's (1982) dichotomizing of psychoanalysis and psychotherapy, will be examined later. Because of their central importance to any distinction among the psychotherapies, the concepts of transference, resistance, and interpretation will be considered specifically and operationally in the next chapter.

CHAPTER 3

Transference, Resistance, and Interpretation

Freud (1913, 1916–1917) defined psychoanalysis technically as a psychotherapy based on the interpretation of transference and resistance. In that transference and resistance are experienced as a dialectic, psychoanalysis and psychoanalytically oriented psychotherapy can be defined as psychotherapies based technically on the interpretation of transference manifestations. The centrality of interpretation of the resistance-transference dialectic in psychoanalytic work demands that the concepts be carefully specified.

TRANSFERENCE

Transference can be understood in a variety of ways depending on which of its aspects is being emphasized. Transference is that component of interpersonal experience from the unacknowledged past that vitally influences one's current view of others and variously determines the nature of any interpersonal interaction (Brenner, 1982). Transference is an integral part of interpersonal experience. It provides stability, predictability, and limitations to the repertoire of one's interpersonal responses.

The basic concept of transference—that interpersonal interaction is influenced by unacknowledged past experiences—is simple and patently true. Yet as the concept is explored, its depth and complexity increase. It is important to emphasize that transference rests on past interpersonal events *as experienced,* that is, as subjectively filtered by phase-specific developmental imperatives. Transference is a chronicle of the subjective aspects of one's interpersonal history, the unconscious, intrapsychic interpersonal accruals that constitute a major component of life experience. To quote Robert Michels, "Although an earlier emphasis in our thinking suggested that transference stood in contrast to reality, the present view would make clear that transference is an essential determinant of all psychic reality. Reality without transference, were it possible, would be less than human" (quoted in Schwaber, 1985, pp. 18–19).

As in interpersonal experience, transference in psychotherapy is generally experienced as actualities in the person of the psychotherapist and the psychotherapeutic procedure. Of the psychotherapies, psychoanalysis and psychoanalytically oriented psychotherapy most assiduously identify and place in dynamic and historical perspective the difference between what is actual in, and what is imposed from the past on, interpersonal relatedness. As Freud (1905b) wrote, "Psycho-analytic treatment does not *create* transference, it merely brings it to light" (p. 117).

The most difficult conceptual issue in understanding transference is the role played by the actual components in the interaction. Freud wrote:

> Some . . . transferences have a content which differs from that of their model in no respect whatever except for the substitution. . . . Others are more ingeniously constructed; their content has been subjected to a moderating influence . . . and they may even become conscious . . . cleverly taking advantage of some real peculiarity in the physician's person or circumstance and attaching themselves to that [p. 116].

To differentiate actual from transferential influences in an interpersonal interaction, the dream as an analogy is useful (Kohut and Seitz, 1963; Bordin, 1974; Bergmann and Hartman, 1976; Gill, 1982).

Although Freud is often thought to have minimized the role of current and actual events in psychic life, in fact he gave new significance to these events by seeing ongoing experience as being in interaction with the past. The essence of Freud's concept, the dynamic unconscious, is the recognition of the interplay of the acknowledged and unacknowledged present with the unacknowledged past. In the interplay, the past, in a sense, continues in the present.

The role of the present in transporting the past into the present is visibly apparent in the dream. In the formation of the dream, Freud called such transporting events the *day residue*. In the dream, the day residue acts essentially as a crossover vehicle by which the past enters the present.

Clinically, the day residue frequently is regarded as merely a vehicle for entering the dream's latent meanings, a view early and strongly argued against by Erikson (1954). As an artifact of clinical presentation, reality is frequently rendered trivial. In fact, the study of the role of the dream residue in dream formation exemplifies the theoretical importance and clinical usefulness of studying the interrelation of the overt and the covert in all aspects of mental functioning.

In fact, it was in describing the capacity of a current event to "call up" the past in the formation of the dream that Freud (1900) first used the term *transference*. As he wrote:

> It must be that [day residues] are essential ingredients in the formation of dreams, since experience has revealed the surprising fact that in the content of every dream some link with a recent daytime impression—often of the most insignificant sort—is to be detected. We learn . . . that an unconscious idea is as such quite incapable of entering the preconscious and that it can only exercise any effect there by establishing a connection with an idea which already belongs to the preconscious, by *transferring* its intensity onto it and by getting itself "covered" by it. Here we have the fact of "*transference*," which provides an explanation of so many striking phenomena in the mental life. . . . [pp. 562–563, italics added].

These crossovers in the dream provide continuing potential for ongoing reworking and integration of the conscious and unconscious past in the context of the present. In the dream past and present become a dialectic—a good model for understanding transference.

The role of the attributes and actions of the psychotherapist in the formation of transference manifestations can be compared to the day residue and its role in providing form and content to the dream. As Edward Bordin (1974) described it,

To the extent that transference and dream phenomena represent primary
process phenomena, one might expect that . . . realistic clues regarding the
analyst are woven into the transferences in the same way that realistic
occurrences are woven into the patient's dreams in the form of "day residue"
[p. 13].

Yet there is a major difference. The dreamer may experience the
dream as completely determined by the previous day's event,
Freud's "dreams from above," or the dreamer may be barely aware
of the relation of the day's event to the dream and be amazed to
discover the initiating or linking events. In interpersonal situations
including psychotherapy, other than after considerable interpreta-
tive work, the interaction seldom is experienced as but actual,
"from above." Although the actual interpersonal components
seemingly dominate the interaction, they, like the day residue,
dynamically "call up" fragments of and conglomerations of interpersonal experience from the past. The transferential is embedded as
a dialectic in the actual. To quote Herman Nunberg (1951), ". . .
transference is like Janus, two-faced, with one face turned to the
past, the other to the present. Through transference the patient lives
the present in the past and the past in the present . . ." (p. 5). The
transference is not in linear relation with time; it is at once a spatial
and a temporal concept (Schwaber, 1985). Like the unconscious
(and the dream), transference does not "know" time.

Freud (1900) used an analogy to the sun and stars to illustrate that
conscious mental life only apparently dominates mental life. Referring to dreams, he wrote, "Dreams give way before the impressions
of a new day just as the brilliance of the stars yields to the light of the
sun" (p. 45). The simile equally illustrates that the actualities in
interpersonal experience eclipse underlying transferential expressions. Like the sun and stars, both actualities and transferential
expressions are there, each influencing the other.

Freud's (1905b) later, more refined clinical view of transference
was developed after his patient Dora prematurely terminated her
psychoanalysis—the earliest recorded systematic study of the unfortunate result of missed transference interpretation. As Freud
wrote,

What are transferences? They are new editions or facsimiles of the impulses
and phantasies which are aroused and made conscious during the progress of

the analysis; but they have this peculiarity . . . , that they replace some earlier person by the person of the physician. To put it another way: a whole series of psychological experiences are revived, not as belonging to the past, but as applying to the person of the physician at the present moment [p. 116].

[In the case of Dora], . . . I was deaf to this first note of warning, thinking I had ample time before me. . . . In this way the transference took me unawares, and . . . she took revenge on me as she wanted to take her revenge on him, and deserted me as she believed herself to have been deceived and deserted by him [p. 119].

Even when interpersonal events and the transference manifestly coincide, the dynamic and ontogenetic structures underlying each are different and can be interpreted (Hoffman, 1983). For example, when a patient comments that he or she fears that the psychotherapist's mind has wandered, rather than confirming, denying, or asking questions about the patient's observation ("How do you feel about that?" questions), the psychotherapist attempts to increase the patient's understanding (offers an interpretation) of possible transferential significances of the patient's observation. If the patient's complaint occurs in the context of an anticipated interruption of the psychotherapy, for instance, the psychotherapist can point out, "Many times you may have thought my mind was wandering. I wonder if you comment on it now because of our impending interruption?"[1]

Paradoxically, along with progressive identification and interpretation of transference comes increasing enactment (regression) of transferences in the psychotherapeutic interaction, unfortunately sometimes spilling over as interactions outside the psychotherapy. It is this increasingly regressive, usually intermittent, enactment in the sessions—the transference neurosis—that gives transference its iatrogenic quality.[2] Such a view regards transference and transfer-

---

[1]Gill commented that he would "try to find out what in the interaction between the patient and me had led to the patient's idea that my mind was wandering. . . . [Y]our making the interpretation you do assumes that you know what it is in the interaction that is responsible [the impending interruption]. . . . I place more emphasis on searching for what in the interaction is, from the patient's point of view, making the patient's transference plausible." I believe Gill's carefulness in this regard reflects a finer technique and that his criticism is warranted.

[2]The term transference neurosis comes from the early psychoanalytic topographical model of conscious, preconscious, and unconscious. The transference

ence neurosis as a continuum reflecting shifting predominance of covert aspects of the relationship. A more useful term than transference neurosis is the generic term regressive transference enactment.[3] Regressive transference enactments encompass a broader range of transference manifestations, reflecting many developmentally related psychopathologies that can be treated psychoanalytically.

The role of "analytic deprivation" in unveiling the transference is complex. Silence should not be equated with "analytic deprivation." As Francois Roustang (1983) sensitively wrote,

> [If] the analyst decides to be silent [and] . . . not risk letting anything . . . appear through gestures or simple movements of his face or hands . . . this procedure is not as effective as it might appear at first: it fails to take into account that silence is a language that the patient learns quickly. There is such an abyss between the silence of death and that of life, such a difference between the silence of inattention and that of alert interest, between the silence of desire and that of impotence, between that of depression and that of continuous mania! Every silence has an intensity and a coloration that is perceptible to the patient. If punctuation gives meaning to a sentence, then surely silence alone, with all its nuances, is capable of passing to the patient all sorts of preconscious or unconscious messages, which are all the more clear because the analyst thinks he is protected from communicating them [p. 59].

The psychotherapist's silence does not produce transference except of a specific kind. Yet interactional responsiveness keeps transferential issues obscure. What is necessary to bring transference into consistent profile is "analytic responding," interactive deprivation with interpretation of the interaction.

The prediction of the degree to which regressive transference enactments, including transference neurosis and psychotic transference distortions, are confined to the psychotherapeutic sessions

---

neurosis was seen as a reexperiencing and reenacting of early childhood conflicts, the repressed childhood neurosis "erupting," so to speak, into consciousness. This scheme emphasizes oedipal achievement and well-established repression barriers.

[3]The term regressive transference enactment is derived from the structural metapsychological model (id, ego, and superego) with emphasis on integrated structuralization, intra- and intersystemic conflicts, and multiple substructures and developmentally related distortions in self- and object representations.

and, more importantly, can be interpreted and the understanding integrated—that is, the prediction of analyzability—is imprecise. Viewed broadly, analyzability cuts across the nosological categories and is related to complex factors embedded in the patient-psychotherapist dyad.

PRIMARY TRANSFERENCE AND THE THERAPEUTIC ALLIANCE

The therapeutic alliance comprises some of the most superficial aspects and some of the most profound influences on the psychotherapeutic relationship. The analogy of the dream to the study of transference—seeing the actual components of the interaction as activating the latent, past interpersonal components—can usefully be employed to understand the therapeutic alliance.

The broad developmental view of the transference that I propose makes transference the bedrock on which all interpersonal relatedness rests. Hans Loewald in a panel discussion of transference (cited in Valenstein, 1974) suggested, "Transference . . . in its most basic meaning has reference to the individual's love life, the source and crux of his psychic development, in both its object-libidinal and its narcissistic aspects" (p. 312). Arthur Valenstein (1974) added,

> The concept of transference relates to the earliest biopsychological determinants . . . those aspects of patient response which do not find their way into articular expression; not just because they are blocked by the resistance of acting out the transference, whether in an analytic situation as such or outside of it, but also because they may not be verbally available to the patient, as a matter of development [p. 313].

The early nonverbal, preoedipal experiencing of other is the developmental foundation, as Phyllis Greenacre (1954) puts it, of the "basic transference, . . . a matrix" upon which relatedness to other in the most fundamental sense develops. When events are propitious, such protoexperience, the unthought known (Bollas, 1987), becomes organized and integrated into Erikson's (1959) basic trust. For the individual, such protoexperience becomes the primal relationship—Donald Winnicott's (1965) holding environment. In psychotherapy, it becomes the *primal* transference (Bibring, 1937; Greenacre; 1954; Zetzel, 1956, 1965). The primal transference in psychotherapy reflects the fundamental relationship to the primal other.

On the highest level, Edward Bibring's (1937) emphasis on an alliance between the psychotherapist and the "healthy part" of the patient's ego captures the sometimes fleeting but generally overriding awareness of the professional, helping component in the psychotherapeutic relationship. Elizabeth Zetzel's (1956) "therapeutic alliance" and Ralph Greenson's (1965) "working alliance" are important but problematic elaborations of Bibring's concept.

Zetzel's therapeutic alliance is closely associated with her strong recommendation for supportive techniques for patients with severe ego impairment. Her aims were therapeutic rather than psychoanalytic, in keeping with her view of the rather limited range of patients who were seen as being able to use interpretation and her limited goals for "sicker" patients. She endorsed a variety of propitious fostering, endorsing, and counseling interventions consistent with her emphasis on helping and strengthening concept. She was a master interactive psychotherapist of the very ill.

Greenson's working alliance accurately reflected his technique. In general, he was little aware of, or at least little concerned about, the ultimate complications of interactive inducement at any stage in psychoanalytic work. His commendable tendency to present his interventions and the patient's responses in his lectures and writing confirms that he was a skillful interactive psychotherapist unimpressed with the importance of insight and acutely aware of techniques for bringing about desired change. In this regard, although Greenson would not agree, he did not much differentiate between interactive psychotherapy and psychoanalysis.

A more inclusive view of the formalities of the psychotherapeutic interplay is Robert Langs's (1978) "frame." Unfortunately, Langs conceptually, and therefore technically, dichotomized frame and transference. His dichotomizing led Langs to "handle" (interact with) crucial aspects of the transference that he assigned to being "frame" issues while interpreting aspects that he considered transference issues. He, in effect, established the patient's conduct for psychotherapy. The patient was made to fit the requirements of the psychotherapy. His choosing which aspects to respond to in which way added interactive elements that overrode the psychoanalytic orientation he otherwise attempted to maintain. In effect, Langs deprived the patient of opportunities for dynamic and genetic insight through working through of crucial transference interactions wrongly regarded, at least in my view, as "frame" issues.

The psychotherapeutic alliance is the primary transference, manifesting itself as a condensation (to continue the analogy to the dream) of the highest and the lowest aspects of the interaction. Jeanne Lampl–De Groot (1975), in her discussion of the working alliance, also used a two-layered concept. She noted that the working alliance stems from the narcissistic object tie with the mother that manifests itself in higher level derivatives such as the feeling of being helped by a professional. Lampl–De Groot contrasted this basis of the working alliance with the basis of the transference, which she saw as developmentally later, ambivalent object-libidinal ties to the parents.

Francois Roustang (1983), using a different frame of reference, also defines levels of transference. Reviving Freud's (1933) term "direct psychical transference," Roustang asked,

> . . . if the relation between analyst and patient makes childhood passion, and the connection to the mother re-emerges, then does not "the direct psychical transference" constitute the cement that analysis proper can never totally lift away or dissolve? One can even wonder whether the analysis of the transference is not likely to reinforce "direct psychical transference" while it appears to undo it [p. 58].

The patient's overriding confidence in the analyst as a professional attempting to help is not physicianly expectation and the cognitive event that the concept working alliance implies. Rather, this confidence is a high-level manifestation of primary transference. Paradoxically and simultaneously, the special importance the patient attaches to selected and overdetermined physical components of the sessions—the hour, office furnishings (especially those that are potentially revealing of the psychotherapist's interests such as pictures and room arrangement), and highly subjectively experienced aspects of the psychotherapist such as manner and voice tone—are derivatives of early kinesthetic components of primary caretaking, cryptic manifestations of primary transference.

These silent but profound attachments to the psychotherapist, which tend to be invisible in the interaction, are brought into bold relief by changes in appointment hours, office moves, and changes in the psychotherapist's voice and manner related to mood and other fluctuating personal impingements. To the surprise of the psychotherapist and the patient, even a well-integrated patient can angrily lament, "You gave away my 3:30 hour," mourn for pictures that have been removed, or feel uneasy with even minimal furniture rearrangements.

Taking the position that the psychotherapeutic alliance is a manifestation of the primary transference raises the question of whether the psychotherapeutic alliance is induced or cultivated (Greenson, 1965, 1967); openly seduced (Roth, 1987); or facilitated by procedural interdicts regarding scheduling, fees, insurance, and the like (Langs, 1978). On close scrutiny, there is no structural difference between the psychotherapeutic alliance and the transference; they are on a continuum of manifestations. Both are omnipresent, although distorted by a variety of primary and secondary factors, loosely considered secondary transferences. Both are revealed and deepen in complexity as resistances, specifically transference resistances, are identified and interpreted and the understanding integrated. Both can be approached identically, that is, through interpretation of resistances as transferentially manifested. This view is similar to that proposed by Charles Brenner (1979): "[The] therapeutic and working alliance . . . refer [sic] to aspects of the transference [and] neither deserve a special name or require special treatment" (p. 136).

If the psychotherapist adopts the view advocated by Greenson (1967) and Roth (1987), that to initiate psychotherapy, the psychotherapeutic alliance must be induced through condoning attitudes and facilitating comments, the psychotherapy from the beginning develops an underlying interactive quality. Rather than early identification of and interpretation of the transference resistance that reveals and intensifies the transference, such inducing interventions impede and obfuscate the transference and increase the potential for identification and certain lower order internalizations of the psychotherapist. These risks are increased through Langs's (1978) "handling" of frame considerations. Because of the Procrustean nature of Langs's recommendations, his methods carry the additional risks of early rupture of the psychotherapy because of under interpretation of and overinterdiction regarding transference resistances or intensification of compliance patterns.

Primary Transference and Tumultuous Transference

Impaired primary transference manifests as tumultuous transference; chaotic interactions, with intense, hostile dependence; severe regressive fusing; destructive and violent behavior; and transient or prolonged lapses into psychosis. Freud's (1914b) differentiation of functional mental "illness" into the transference neuroses (psychoneuroses, perhaps better termed the structural neuroses [Valenstein, 1985]), and the narcissistic neuroses (psychoses) had paradigmatic importance. Freud used the *nature* of the transference rather than nosological symptom constellations as the prime diagnostic differentiating factor.[4] Yet as noted by Wallerstein (cited in Peltz, 1987), it was ". . . a major theoretical and clinical error [of Freud to consider] psychotics [as] incapable of forming transferences . . ." (p. 695). Essentially Freud (1914b) confused chaotic (that is, severely developmentally distorted) transference with lack of transference. Freud's view is correct if transference is narrowly defined as the displacement of differentiated, integrated object representations from the past onto related or unrelated differentiated, integrated object representations in the present. When transference is broadly defined as the distorting of the experiencing of objects in the present by object representations from the past, however distorted (that is, unintegrated part- and polarized object representations), Freud's view is limited. Obviously, such distinctions reach vast importance when one considers the regressive transference enactments in psychoanalytic work with borderlines and psychotics.

Questions regarding the availability of primary transference to

---

[4]Freud's reliance on the nature of transference for diagnostic purposes fits well into clinical practice. Most psychoanalytically oriented psychotherapists unknowingly rely on the transference diagnostically both nosologically and for analyzability. Beyond transference considerations as evaluated by the psychotherapist are many subtle factors related to patient–psychotherapist "fit" that cut across nosological evaluation and make analyzability difficult to predict. Considerations regarding analyzability complement but do not replace nosological evaluation, which is of great demographic importance.

interpretation are difficult to answer. Generally interpretation of the primary transference takes the form of making observations on behavior—a process of making verbally overt what is behaviorally covert. Such "putting into words" is part of the many interactive aspects of the psychotherapy. Transcending what is said, the psychotherapist becomes a person who verbalizes rather than acts. Although providing the "high-level" model of talking rather than acting (a "value" often indiscriminately promoted in psychotherapy offices), such verbalizing on a lower level is tantamount to primary soothing (the mother's voice), closely related to kinesthetic sensations including physical rocking and containment. Such soothing, as experienced particularly by a severely disturbed ego and to some extent by all egos, is significantly different from other interactive interventions and may be "beyond interpretation" (Gedo, 1979, 1981). As with all interpretive interventions, there are interactive concomitants (Stone, 1961). Yet a distinction must be maintained between "talking" to soothe and talking about the experience of being talked to as being soothing.

Exploring the interplay between words and sensations, Roustang (1983) elaborated on Freud's (1905c) comment, ". . . for the words of our everyday discourse are nothing other than faded magic." Roustang continued,

> If there is a place where words have been restored to their magical power, above and beyond what they can attain in the doctor–patient relation, it is surely in analytic treatment. . . . This is because the analyst's words have a power that everyday discourse lacks, . . . that they can produce analytic effects, or in Freud's words, . . . that they will lead to "the patient's independence." But precisely because they do have a magical power, they cannot avoid having, on the other hand, the inverse effect of linking the patient more closely to the analyst [who wanted to free him] The words become the medium of communication between unconscious minds [pp. 58–59].

It may be that the nature of the primary transference in a particular patient is the pivotal consideration determining whether the psychotherapy, be it psychoanalytically oriented psychotherapy or psychoanalysis, becomes essentially an interactive psychotherapy regardless of the psychotherapist's intent. Even so, because of the tendency on the part of psychotherapists, including psychoanalytically oriented psychotherapists, toward interactional gratification, tendencies closely related to Freud's (1915, 1916–1917) cautions regarding patients' desires to be "treated" with transferences, there is a danger that many patients, including markedly disturbed patients, will be "sold short," that is, deprived of the opportunity psychoanalytically to achieve personality changes of greater scope and depth (Balint, 1966; Oremland, 1972). In psychoanalytically oriented psychotherapy with any patient, the better is invariably the enemy of the good. In interactive psychotherapy, the better is the good.

It is important to make explicit that it is fully recognized that all interventions, including interpretations, carry complex transferential, interactional components and gratifications. The point is that such gratifications are not the aim of the psychotherapist, nor are they manipulated toward goals. Rather, such interactional components are complexities that must be ferreted out, identified, and interpreted to the degree that they can be. The analysis of the interaction, including the interventions, is the difference between the interactive and the psychoanalytic orientation. In short, the psychoanalytic orientation is an ideal to be strived for but rarely fully achieved.

Resistance

Resistance is differentiated from defense. Defenses are conscious and unconscious maneuvers—intellectualizations, identifications, isolations, and, at a lower level of functioning, projection, negation, reaction formation, and splitting—that determine characteristic ways of adapting, evaluating, and attributing. Defenses are part of character development, character pathology, and symptom formation. The higher order defenses, including the various internalizations, are integrally related to developmental interpersonal experience. Lower order defenses, such as negation, denial, reaction formation, and splitting, are less integral to interpersonal experience and are more a part of endopsychic homeostatic functioning.

As a concept, defense derives from the structural and topographic models of psychic functioning and is easily reified in clinical and theoretical discussions. Much of how psychotherapy is spuriously described, particularly prescriptions for supportive interventions, rests on reified concepts of defense derived from the major psychoanalytic models of the mind. The directive to reinforce defenses, particularly nonpathological defenses (with all the hidden value judgments and tendencies toward a mean socialization that are implied), is derived from topographic models, for example, thinking of "the unconscious about to erupt." A reified view of the structural model may lead to the imprecise recommendation that the psychotherapist "strengthen ego boundaries" or "become an auxiliary ego" for the patient. "Becoming an auxiliary ego" more accurately captures the importance of defective and distorted internalizations (introjects and identifications) in a class of psychopathology and is an attempt to intervene interactively than does the less specific and less meaningful directive to "strengthen ego boundaries," which is derived from a reification of the structural model.

In contrast to defense, resistance is a phenomenon of psychotherapy that strongly carries interpersonal connotations. In psychoanalytically oriented psychotherapy, by moving the patient in a direction toward greater awareness, the psychotherapist's interventions activate the patient's resistance (the desire to maintain the intrapsychic status quo) manifested in the transference.[5] Resistance is a condensation of characteristic constellations of defenses and transferences enacted in the psychotherapeutic interaction; resistance and transference are essentially a dialectic.

Although manifested as an interpersonal tug of war, transference resistance is an externalization of internal struggles. When verbalized, the patient's expectations of how the psychotherapist will react as contents are revealed become the linchpin for distinguishing between the patient's experiencing of and the actualities of the interaction. Recognition of this discrepancy, at times initiated by the patient and at other times initiated by the psychotherapist is the window of the transference, the first step in the process of

---

[5]Roy Schafer (1976) writes about resisting rather than resistance. His insistence on verb rather than nominative forms, an action language, is more than a semantic difference. He attempts to make the language of psychoanalysis correspond closely to personality functioning. Yet clinical discussions continue to employ the reified and anthropomorphic nominative forms.

interpreting the transference. The technical adage "interpret defense before impulse" is true but not in the way usually implied; more accurately stated, the adage should be, begin by interpreting resistance within the transference contents. To illustrate, the interpretive intervention, "You are afraid for me to know you"—as opposed to interactive interventions such as "Tell me your thoughts" or asking a leading question—can begin the interpretation of the silence. The interpretive "It's safer if I tell you about me than for you to tell me about you," as opposed to the interactive reflecting back a patient's question, can bring about an exploration of the patient's defensive questioning of the psychotherapist.

Interpretation

The process of reaching an interpretation, the intervention central to any technical definition of the psychoanalytic orientation, involves a variety of interventions (Glover, 1955, Bibring, 1954; Gedo, 1979, 1981). Bibring (1954) in particular identified the place of questions and clarifications in the process of developing interpretations. Such preliminary activities, closely akin to interactions, may have strong therapeutic effects, which, working in lieu of interpretation, in effect make the psychotherapy interactive rather than psychoanalytic. Glover (1955) was a master of using preliminary interventions psychotherapeutically.

The term interpretation first appeared in psychoanalysis in the title of Freud's (1900) most important work, *The Interpretation of Dreams.* Freud's description was simple and encompassing:

> ... "interpreting" a dream implies assigning a "meaning" to it—that is, replacing it by something which fits into the chain of our mental acts as a link having a validity and importance equal to the rest [p. 96].

> [Psychoanalytic interpretation] might be described as ... [a] *"decoding"* method, since it treats dreams as a kind of cryptography in which each sign can be translated into another sign having a known meaning. . . . The essence of the decoding procedure ... lies in the fact that the work of interpretation is not brought to bear on the dream as a whole but on each portion of the dream's content independently, as though the dream were a geological conglomerate in which each fragment of rock required a separate assessment [pp. 97–99].

In a footnote referring to the second-century Artemidorus of Daldis, Freud revealed his awareness that it is within the patient's contexts and thoughts that the information for decoding the cryptographs is found, a paradigmatic change in method for decoding learned from his studies of hysterical symptoms.

Freud's definition of psychoanalytic interpretation is close to the ordinary English definition of the word interpretation. In the *Third Webster's Unabridged Edition,* interpretation is defined as "to explain the meaning of." Webster's expanded definition includes "to bring out the meaning of, especially to give one's own conception of."

Interpretation in psychoanalysis and psychoanalytically oriented psychotherapy involves inferences drawn from what is being said, felt, and enacted by the patient. The model is the understanding of the "meaning" of the hysterical symptom as symbolic somatic expressions are translated into words according to psychoanalytic concepts. Such inferences, when refined, coalesced, and verbalized, are called an interpretation. *A psychoanalytic interpretation is a concise, integrated inference regarding the meanings and motivations of emotional, verbal, and behavioral expressions in terms of psychoanalytic theories of development, psychodynamics, and psychopathology.* Interpretation, by adding meaning to what is being experienced, is the most supportive and least regression inducing of the therapeutic interventions.

Because most information about the meanings and motivations of transference enactments comes from the psychotherapist's empathic experiencing and countertransference awareness, inferences regarding the transference are the most valid of all areas of psychoanalytic investigation. We know more about what is going on between the patient and the psychotherapist in the psychotherapeutic interaction than what is going on between the patient and any other person in any other situation, present or past. In that the interaction between patient and psychotherapist is an alive, dynamic integration of past and present, it is potentially the most convincing area for exploration. Psychoanalytically oriented psychotherapy is a vital exploration of the psychodynamics of the patient and the psychotherapist interaction—the true and immediate "here and now."

The place of genetic or developmental and reconstructive interpretation in psychoanalysis and psychoanalytically oriented psychotherapy—the origins of character traits and pathology—is complex, difficult to establish, and even more difficult to validate.

Reconstructive statements come largely from the patient, not the psychotherapist, and are partly confirmatory response and, paradoxically, partly resistance to transference-centered interpretations. Genetic statements by the patient further the work in the sense that the information adds new dimensions and are attempts to move the "field" of inquiry from the present to the past—resistance in the broad sense. The psychotherapist further interprets the new information from the past and helps refine and increase the scope of understanding of past in the present. Mindful of the temptation to both patient and psychotherapist to move from the immediacy of the interaction to surmises about remote events, the psychotherapist interweaves the themes of the past with the themes of the present, each enriching the understanding of the other.

When the psychotherapist is dubious, as is frequently the case, the style of interpretation reflects that dubiousness. When the psychotherapist is certain, the phrasing reflects that certainty. The psychotherapist does not artificially soften observations, effect a hesitant posture, ask leading questions, attempt to persuade, try to get the patient thinking about things, grunt acknowledgment, or model for the patient. Such interactive interventions confound rather than clarify the transference. Head nodding and adding to the conversation, although subject to misinterpretation by the patient, are indications of attempts to understand rather than attempts at being conducive. The overriding principle is that the psychotherapist does not effect a style for interactive purposes.

Interpretive statements are generally taken by the patient interactively in the context of the transference. The interpretations become transferentially distorted by the patient into instructions, rebuffs, criticism, and the like. As such responses are identified, the distortions become the object of the subsequent investigation. The psychotherapy becomes a continuing process initiated by the patient's comments and actions, developed by the psychotherapist's interpretations, modified by the patient often with genetic clarification, and further refined by the psychotherapist's interpretive responses and the patient's additions as an interpretive line develops. For example, the psychotherapist's lack of response to a question may elicit from the patient, "You are trying to get me to think of it myself?" The psychotherapist interprets, "You're justifying me to protect me from your anger." Perhaps the patient then falls silent, and the psychotherapist continues, "You withhold from me the way you felt I withheld from you—a kind of anger." The patient responds, "If I get angry, you won't talk to me." The psychotherapist responds, "You see me as easily frightened by your feelings and clamming up to punish you."

Any discussion of the centrality of interpretation to the psychoanalytic orientation returns us to Gill's (1954) affirmation that the resolution of the transference in psychoanalysis is "by interpretation alone." Resolution essentially means that important and lasting shifts in perspective on self- and object representations are achieved through the psychodynamic and genetic understanding of what is being experienced in the transference. Yet there is a curious redundancy in Gill's phrase "by techniques of interpretation alone." There is no other way for transference to be resolved other than by interpretation. All other interventions allow for additions to, but not essential changes in, the fundaments of transference; in fact, they embalm the transference (Eissler, 1953, 1958; Roustang, 1983). Further, we know that even in optimal psychoanalytic circumstances, the resolution of the transference is only partial and the potential for regressive transference manifestations lives on (Norman et al., 1976).

John Gedo (1979, 1981) has eloquently stated that although the essence of psychoanalysis lies in the interpretation of the transference, interventions other than interpretation bring transference into clear profile. On this matter, Gedo and I disagree. Part of the disagreement may be in defining interpretation, which I do more broadly than he. Regardless of differences in definition, Gedo is broader than I in his view of how interactive one can be—in fact, at times must be—in order to interpret the transference, which Gedo defines more narrowly than I.

CONFRONTATION AND INTERDICTION

If psychoanalytic interpretation is considered as a process of making psychoanalytic inferences from the patient's narrative, form of communication, and behavior, the distinction between interpretation and confrontation rapidly disappears. Yet there are clinical reasons to maintain a distinction between inferences based on material that has strong preconscious representation, interpretation, and those based on material with more distant preconscious representation, confrontation. Viewed this way, confrontation is a matter not of style of presentation but of the "distance" between the awareness and the behavior about which inferences are being made.

Generally, confrontations are inferences about acting out, behavior that is, by definition, designed to keep thoughts and feelings out of conscious awareness. Confrontation—verbalization of an inference, usually about behavior when the patient's awareness (preconscious representation) is minimal—is among the most difficult, most risky, and at times the most essential of the interpretive interventions that the psychotherapist has to make in psychoanalytically oriented psychotherapy.

Our theoretical understanding of acting out is largely based on Freud's (1914a) paper, "Remembering, Repeating, and Working-Through." In clinical work, acting out varies from extraordinarily subtle intrasession behaviors, such as facile insightfulness, to gross, life-threatening enactments outside the sessions. Lateness, a large variety of errors regarding appointments and payment, cancellation of appointments, discussing the psychotherapy with others, initiating a host of new behaviors, relationships, and activities are but some of the enormous repertory of acting-out behaviors that must be evaluated and systematically "confronted" by the psychotherapist.

Interestingly, often an omission is in itself evidence of acting out. Discovering and confirming omissions requires highly skillful transference and countertransference consideration by the psychotherapist. For example, a patient who is thinking about a job change that requires a move—itself a difficult action to evaluate from the standpoint of acting out—may, in making a list of the advantages and disadvantages, leave psychotherapy off the list. The psychotherapist must then confront the patient with something like, "I notice that psychotherapy is not on the list of things that will be drastically changed by such a move." When the list includes psychotherapy but minimizes the relationship with the psychotherapist, the psychotherapist must at times point out, "You talk about me as though I were easily replaceable." Seemingly paradoxically, high estimation as well as minimalization of the psychotherapist's importance must be interpreted; otherwise only "negative" aspects of the transference are subject to interpretation. *A psychotherapy that interprets negative transference and "fosters" positive transference is interactive psychotherapy.*

Because of patients' lack of awareness, confronting them with the centrality of the transference in their behavior often gives psychotherapists the uneasy feeling, frequently aided by patients' accusations, that they see themselves as overly important in the patients' lives. This feeling, an important countertransference manifestation, is a common inhibitor of transference interpretation. Psychotherapists may resist transference-oriented interpretation because of countertransferential tendencies to overestimate their own importance to their patients. A full understanding of transference requires that psychotherapists have a full sense of their limited role as persons—as opposed to their role as transference figures—in the psychotherapeutic interaction. It is the struggle against that sense of absence of self in the transference manifestations that forces psychotherapists to feel defensively overly important to the patients, paradoxically inhibiting full transference awareness. These considerations, which are closely related to the psychotherapists' narcissistic needs and vulnerabilities, make it difficult for psychotherapists to differentiate the transferential from the actual.

Lampl-De Groot (1976) made exactly the opposite point. Warning of the dangers of extreme devotion to transference interpretation, she opined that psychoanalysts could overestimate their importance to patients with the result that the psychoanalysis would be aggrandized and external life belittled. I believe that hers is an overly narrow view of transference that does not appreciate the degree to which "external life" is part of the material and actualities of the transference. The same can be said of Anna Freud's (1965) comment, "If [the psychoanalyst] is too eager to see . . . all current happenings in terms of transference and of resistance . . . their value in reality [is discounted]" (p. 50).

Unfortunately like many clinical concepts, the term acting out has been expanded unsystematically to include, in addition to the acting out of transference-activated thoughts, a wide variety of impulsive behaviors, antisocial behaviors, and behaviors generally condemned by the psychotherapist. The acknowledgment of, and bringing to the patient's attention, the consequences of various impulsive behavior are various kinds of *interdictions*, which are interactions rather than confrontations. Such interdictions, combined with varying amounts of explanation of consequences, are in structure markedly different from confrontation, the interpretation of the meaning of the behavior as transferential enactment, acting out narrowly defined.

ANNOUNCEMENTS

Psychotherapists at times must bring to their patients information regarding items or events that are not related to the ongoing flow of material. Adjustments of schedule, interruptions, fee changes, various kinds of information received about patients such as insurance requests, and the like are important components of the psychotherapeutic interaction. To be avoided in psychoanalytically oriented psychotherapy are such statements as "Before we begin, I should tell you. . . ." These statements indicate an unsupportable view by the psychotherapist that there is material "inside" and "outside" the hour and establishes artificial boundaries to the material and what is to be responded to.

In the well-conducted psychoanalytic psychotherapy practice, announcements are infrequent and the psychotherapist has innumerable opportunities to listen to the free flow of material. In psychoanalytically oriented psychotherapy, it is best to deal with announcements as special events of the psychotherapy and allow the most time to deal with them, that is, to make them at the beginning of the hour. Although making announcements at the beginning of the session does interfere with the flow material, it has the advantage, in addition to allowing the psychotherapist maximal time to work with the response to the announcement or lack of it, of keeping the announcement free of the contamination inherent when an announcement comes during the session. For example, if a patient begins a session with "I can't see you next week," it is difficult for the psychotherapist at that moment to announce an interruption without seeming to be (in fact, he may be) retaliating for the patient's announcement.

On occasion the psychotherapist may regret making an announcement at the beginning because the patient may follow by reporting some stunning bad news. Such unfortunate coincidence is rare, and it is generally advisable to make announcements at the beginning of the session.

Karl Menninger (1936) took a diametrically opposite stand and urged practitioners to make announcements at the end of the hour to preserve the integrity of the hour as being patient initiated.[6] According to Menninger, "The analyst who 'begins' a patient's hour by an announcement violates his own statement of wanting to hear the spontaneous free association material of the patient's mind. It is bad manners, and it is a technical error" (p. 40). Beyond stating that the analyst was violating his own statement, Menninger did not discuss the theoretical basis for preserving the integrity of every hour as being patient initiated; nor did Menninger discuss the problems created by announcements presented in such a way that they cannot be responded to until the next hour. Menninger's presentation at the end of sessions may carry the implication that material is "inside" or "outside" the hour. Thus, it encourages an artificial separation of what is and what is not to be analyzed. From an interactive point of view, presenting material when it cannot be responded to models for the patient that important material can be "dropped" at the end to avoid responding to it or to shift the responsibility for initiating discussion to the psychotherapist. Of course, such "dropping" can be interpreted in the next session, but interpretation is difficult when the psychotherapist is exemplifying a way of dealing with the material.

Gill (personal communication) has noted, "I think it is desirable to wait a moment or two to make sure that the patient is not bursting with something that he must bring out." Gill's proposal

---

[6]Patient initiated refers to the practice in psychoanalysis and psychoanalytically oriented psychotherapy of waiting in each session for the patient to begin the discourse. This practice is theoretically validated by the fact that the first words, as they are selected from the myriad of thoughts, become overdetermined and transferentially laden. To enhance the overdetermination in the selection, most psychoanalytically aware practitioners are neutral and parsimonious in how they greet patients at each session.

does not circumvent the problem of the announcement's being "tied" to the patient's initial material and of its therefore being construed as a response to the material, or that it is part of counter-transference enactment.

That three experienced practitioners differ in their recommendations regarding such a technical point as when to make an announcement has a yet greater significance: Although students would like unanimity in the application of basic principles, the greater lesson is that students must learn to evaluate the theoretical rationale behind technical recommendations (such as making announcements, fee setting, dealing with canceled appointments, and the like). Students should not adopt a procedure because it seems right, is advanced by a respected authority, or, as is, unfortunately, most often the case, it was the way their own psychoanalysts or psychotherapists proceeded.

In psychoanalytically oriented psychotherapy interruptions are referred to simply as interruptions. "I won't be able to see you between such and such" provides the necessary information and is open ended enough to allow maximal response by the patient. It is unwise to label interruptions even when they are positive, such as vacations. Labeling certain interruptions becomes interactive suggestion, at times, conscious modeling. Such labeling also leaves the psychotherapist with the problem of what to say regarding "bad" interruptions such as those for illness or family problems. Basically, the most associative use can be made of an announcement of an interruption when it is as free of suggestive contents as possible. This method best preserves the opportunity to deal with the responses within the widest transferential context.

Interruptions, which psychoanalytically are attenuated abandonments—not necessarily universally unwelcome by the patient—are so heavily freighted with transference and countertransference responses that it is generally better for the psychotherapist to decide on a particular time to inform all the patients of an impending interruption. Thus, the psychotherapist has the advantage of not announcing interruptions under the sway of countertransference proclivities. One should not wait for the right time for announcing interruptions; there never is a right time. Moreover, presenting impending interruptions to all patients over a relatively short period of time has the advantage of allowing the psychotherapist to see in broad texture the response to interruption. It provides a curious confirmation of theory regarding the centrality of the transference to see how characteristically and yet individually patients respond.

Single appointment cancellations can be made the previous week if the patient is being seen more than once a week. Generally, longer interruptions, two to three weeks, require at least three to four weeks anticipation. Regressed patients need somewhat more anticipatory time and detailed preparation, including, at times, discussion of arrangements for their being seen by someone else during the interruption.

Although it is easy to misconstrue such descriptions as diminishing spontaneity, the psychotherapist, aware of the meaning of interruptions, must be mindful that both spontaneity and rigidity can reflect countertransference enactment as well as characterological style. In psychoanalytically oriented psychotherapy, the psychotherapist attempts to deal with interruptions in a manner that allows maximal continuity of the psychotherapy while providing maximal opportunity to explore the responses fully.

Because it is obviously advantageous to minimize interruptions, ideally the psychotherapist's and the patient's times away should coincide. Such scheduling requires that the psychotherapist announce longer interruptions as early as possible so that patients can, if possible, make corresponding plans. Respect for the patients' plans requires that the psychotherapist plan as far in advance as possible and becomes one of the many restrictions that the psychotherapist must endure. Although psychotherapists enjoy the fruits of the regularity of a psychotherapy practice, they sacrifice personal flexibility because of its heavily scheduled nature. Unlike other professionals, we in psychoanalytically oriented psychotherapy cannot work a little faster if we want to leave work a little earlier.

EXTRATRANSFERENCE INTERPRETATIONS

A considerable literature has grown regarding interpretation of situations and interactions not directly transferentially related, that is, extratransference interpretations (Strachey, 1934; Brenner, 1976; Lampl-De Groot, 1976; Lietes, 1977; Stone, 1961; Blum,

1983). Although I am strongly supportive of the view that the predominant interventions in psychoanalytically oriented psychotherapy are interpretive and transference centered, I see a place for extratransference interpretations particularly in psychotherapies that are far along. A great asset to keeping interpretation transference centered is the increased accuracy of such interpretations over any others. Yet, over time the psychotherapist becomes familiar with a variety of situations and people in the patient's life, and increasingly valid dynamic interpretations of extratransference circumstances can be offered. Such interventions by the psychotherapist increase in the middle phase. These extratransference interpretations are not to be confused with genetic constructions that are initiated early by the patient in response to interpretation of the transference and are developed and refined in the subsequent interpretive process.

In summary, extraanalytic interpretations suffer from lack of information about the other people involved and are highly subject to inaccuracies and the overriding tendency of extratransference events being used to mitigate and hide the transference. Extratransference interpretation, especially early in the psychotherapy, can itself reflect countertransference "acting out," with competitive, dependency-inducing, and idealization-inducing consequences as the psychotherapist demonstrates a "greater wisdom." In general, extratransference interpretations lend to modeling, identification, and introjective changes rather than to insightful new perspectives and therefore should be used only with informed caution in psychoanalytically oriented psychotherapy.

_____ **CHAPTER 4**

Neutrality,
Countertransference,
and Abstinence

In my exploration of psychoanalytically oriented psychotherapy, I
have emphasized that the cornerstone of the psychoanalytic orientation is interpretation, a translating process that adds levels of
meaning to what is said, implied, and portrayed in the interchange
between the patient and the psychotherapist. The contents of psychoanalytic interpretations are derived from the composite of theories that constitutes the psychoanalytic understanding of dynamics, development, and psychopathology. What develops in the
course of the psychotherapy is a broadening understanding of the
patient's present and past, largely in interpersonal terms, that re-
duces the propensity toward certain repetitive reenactments and to
varying degrees potentiates the future.

This schematic view of what happens in the psychoanalytic
therapeutic process, although accurate, does not, however, address
a primary overriding concern, the ever-present specter of suggestion, whether direct or indirect, through selective attention and
inattention to various factors. The predominance of suggestion is
the major differentiation between the interactive and the psychoanalytically oriented modes.

The subtleties of suggestion are extensively detailed in Francois
Roustang's (1983) study of Freud's interest in telepathy. Roustang
approaches a complex consideration of unconscious communica-

tion, particularly "transmission" from the unconscious of the psychoanalyst to the unconscious of the patient.

> What analytic treatment sets up and what the analyst reinforces . . . is an immediate relationship of an archaic, infantile, erotic sort, the aim of which is the negation of all alterity. . . . The principle of [Freud's] "direct psychical transference" is never to be separated . . . to be one in the other . . . leav[ing] one with] no autonomy [pp. 59–60].

> By this distant interest in telepathy, Freud wants to repudiate the most formidable enemy, and that enemy is suggestion. . . . To admit that the analyst can have an influence on the patient or that he can will or wish something for him . . . would ruin the entire psychoanalytic discovery. . . . above all, one must at any cost prevent such a question from being posed, for if it is posed, one will be forced to speak not only of the analyst's conscious wishes but of his unconscious wishes, which would put him in the position of never really being able to know what he is doing [pp. 55–56].

Roustang ironically concluded, ". . . as long as the transference is well understood and summarized by saying 'That's your problem,' one is sure of protecting analysis from everything that could disturb its purity" (p. 56).

Continuing to use Freud's interest in telepathy as a vehicle for understanding the relation of suggestion to psychoanalysis, Roustang noted that

> telepathy is different from analysis, because the latter seeks to explain how the passage of thought from one person to another takes place and because it wants to establish continuity between the various facts that are presented, while those who adhere to telepathy try to preserve the mysterious and therefore leave all the intermediate elements in the realm of incomprehensibility and strangeness" [p. 54].

Roustang continues, perhaps tongue in cheek, "Psychoanalysis wants to be irrevocably on the side of science and therefore rejects what it cannot account for" (p. 54).

As is emphasized repeatedly, the major corrective to suggestion is the psychotherapist's attention to the identification and the interpretation of the transference. Such attention alone does not answer completely the frequent allegation that psychoanalytically oriented psychotherapy and psychoanalysis are but a subtle, systematic insinuation of a social philosophy. Only research, slow in coming and difficult to validate, can decide this point (Wallerstein, 1986).

TRANSFERENCE/COUNTERTRANSFERENCE

My overriding thesis is that transference, as understood psychoanalytically, is the ubiquitous, rich underpinning that provides a distinctive mark to the way one relates. Such a definition requires recognition of the transference contribution of the psychotherapist, traditionally called the countertransference, to the psychotherapeutic interchange. Countertransferences are regressive manifestations in the psychotherapist—albeit observed and controlled manifestations—in response to the patient's specifics.

The countertransference is best thought of as a subset of transference responses of the psychotherapist in the specific psychotherapy dyad. Such specific responses are momentary or enduring, subtle or overt, easily identifiable or requiring careful self-scrutiny and at times consultation.

Discussion of countertransference raises issues of regression, briefly skirted in the discussion of transference. Regression in psychoanalysis is used spatially and temporally—spatially in the sense of ego and superego regression with concretized thought and primitive defenses, and temporally in the sense that the past overrides the present.

All psychotherapies induce regression, and psychoanalysis is generally considered the most regression inducing of the psychotherapies. The regressive potential in psychoanalysis is paradoxical and complex.[1] Arlow (1975) noted

> . . . that psychoanalytic technique induces regression in the patient . . . is a principle . . . circulated without challenge for a long time. . . . [W]hat the psychoanalytic situation does is to create . . . a set of conditions which permit regressive aspects of the patient's mental functioning, long present, to reemerge in forms that are clearer and easier to observe [p. 73].

In psychoanalysis, the patient is pulled in many directions simultaneously.

---

[1]The apparently interminable, lifelong psychoanalyses, often cited to warn prospective patients away from psychoanalysis, are generally interactive psychotherapies masquerading under the trappings of psychoanalysis. Those who chide, "They will keep you coming forever" are revealing, in projected form, intensely desired and intensely feared enactment of dependency wishes.

In fact, interactive psychotherapy is the most regression inducing of the psychoanalytic psychotherapies. In interactive psychotherapy, transference desires are enacted and in that sense are realized by both psychotherapist and patient and are subjected to selective scrutiny.

The emphasis on transference as the major underpinning of all interpersonal relatedness should not be construed to imply that in psychoanalytically oriented psychotherapy and in psychoanalysis the transferential situations of the patient and the psychotherapist are identical. In both, the patient's responses are at a more fluctuating level of regression than the psychotherapist's.[2] It is the recognition of the generally deeper level of regression in the patient than in the psychotherapist that gives the psychotherapist confidence that regressive phenomena in the interaction are largely transferential. For example, a patient's lateness probably is a regressive transference enactment, whereas the psychotherapist's lateness is probably realistically or characterologically determined. Obviously such a view is easily distorted and abused (Gill, 1982).

The view of countertransference as a contaminant of the psychotherapy, rather than as a valued, important, albeit delicate tool by which the psychotherapist identifies components of the interaction highly relevant to the patient, has been long accepted and well documented (Shane, 1980; Tyson, 1986). By and large psychoanalysis has relied on personal psychoanalysis, continuing self-analysis, and training to elevate countertransference out of its distorting bias into a highly useful therapeutic tool. Ideally, successive generations of psychoanalysts have, through training, come to understand the prerequisite psychoanalytic theories and, through personal psychoanalyses, have become relatively able to identify patterns within themselves that when raised to a higher level by specific patients can be usefully turned into "data," which become part of the contents of the psychotherapist's interpretation of the interaction of the moment.

---

[2]Intensity of regression is, by convention, referred to spatially as depth, reflecting the early topographical model of psychoanalysis. Statements such as "the deep, dark recesses of the mind" or "the child resides deeply inside all of us" reflect the subjective sense of spatial layering, the topography of personal experience.

Although the correctives of training and countertransference awareness work well enough clinically and have become shibboleths of psychoanalytic practice, the question remains whether a higher principle is involved regarding the psychoanalyst's influence. Is it enough to say that through theoretical knowledge, self-awareness, and experience psychoanalysts can recognize specific responses as they are being induced and can bring them to a level at which they can be verbalized as interpretations in the context of the patient's response?[3] The complex phenomena involved in a full understanding of the psychoanalyst's influence bring us to issues of abstinence and neutrality.

Abstinence entered the psychoanalytic lexicon early in the development of technique (Freud, 1916–1917). Whether or not there was a period when psychoanalysis, through its early overestimation and misunderstanding of the role of sexuality in psychopathology, actually required sexual abstinence is not clear, but for a variety of obvious reasons even discussion of the necessity for sexual abstinence for patients in psychoanalysis was soon abandoned. The earliest significant theoretical formulations about abstinence centered on the idea that frustration of specific desires and urges raised anxiety and conflicts surrounding such desires to a greater level of obviousness and hence analyzability. The use of frustration to increase visibility of anxiety and conflict early proved of limited clinical value but was later subtly refined as interpretive, rather than interactive, responsiveness became better understood.

As understanding of the nature of enactment increased, particularly Freud's (1914a) understanding of acting out, abstinence took on new meaning. Psychoanalysis found itself in a situation wherein patients were asked, indirectly and sometimes directly, to abstain from certain acts until the motivations for and consequences of those acts could be analyzed.[4] Generally these edicts were direct

---

[3]Most psychoanalysts so identify with the psychoanalytic view that they and the view are one. Thus, practitioners more often are disciples than students. The last two decades have witnessed important discussions placing psychoanalytic theory into an epistemological perspective, discussions largely ignored by clinicians (Rieff, 1961, 1968; Sulloway, 1979; Schorske, 1981).

[4]Apparently opposite, but actually in the same theoretical vein, Freud (1919) came to encourage phobic patients at a point in their treatment to expose themselves to their specific fears, for example, to ride in an elevator or go to a high place

injunctions against decisions of consequence. Obvious examples included refraining from marriage, divorce, having children, job changes, and the like until the determinants of such decisions could be more fully understood. These requests that the patient consciously keep the "field clean" while psychoanalytic work proceeded came to be the standard level of abstinence for psychoanalysis (Freud, 1915). In fact, in addition to the requests for free association, many psychoanalysts often incorporated cautions regarding consequential actions as part of their initial instruction to the patient.[5]

With the scope of psychoanalytic work increasing, such interdictions grew in importance (Stone, 1954). Eissler (1953, 1958) elevated these interdictions to the level of specific psychoanalytic intervention by defining how they could be employed while maintaining the psychoanalytic orientation. It is no news to any experienced psychotherapist that the capacity to comply with such requests is inversely related to the degree of various characterological and psychopathological difficulties that require the interventions. In some psychotherapies, including psychoanalysis, interdictive

---

to make manifest the anxiety, more precisely the fantasies underlying the anxiety, hidden by avoidance and ego inhibition. As Freud wrote, "[The patient] will never . . . bring into the analysis the material indispensable for a convincing resolution of the phobia. . . . It is only when . . . [patients] struggle with their anxiety while they make the attempt . . . at the physician's demand that the associations and memories come into the patient's mind which enable the phobia to be resolved" (pp. 165–166).

In Freud's descriptions of this specific intervention, the earliest use of parameters, we can see differentiation of a deconditioning interactive intervention (face the phobia to overcome one's fears), a transferential interactive intervention (face the phobia and overcome it so that I will be pleased with you), and a psychoanalytic intervention (face the phobia so that we can analyze the underlying motivations) (Eissler, 1953).

[5]Giving initial instruction to the patient was part of the very beginnings of psychoanalysis and reflected its origins in hypnosis. Yet, the request for or instruction in free association runs counter to psychoanalytic theory. Free association is the aim, not the instrument, of psychoanalysis. Although in psychoanalysis, for the sake of tradition I initially explain and request free association, I know that it is the result of interpretation of resistance. In this regard my psychoanalytically oriented psychotherapy is psychoanalytically purer than my psychoanalysis. Unencumbered by tradition, in psychoanalytically oriented psychotherapy I begin with transference interpretation of the difficulties in thinking and talking freely.

interventions constitute a significant portion of the interventions, particularly in the preliminary phase. These psychotherapies mostly fail.

Searching for a basic principle governing the psychotherapist's behavior akin to patient's abstinence, discussions often lead to recommendations regarding infrequency of interventions, relative silence, and "analytic anonymity." Such descriptive admonishments are quantitative. Although initiated, and still frequently viewed, as the frustration of gratification to increase the patient's anxiety and thus bring conflicts into broader profile, as the bipersonal aspect of psychotherapy has become more fully recognized, analytic anonymity is more accurately seen as a necessity, parallel to the patient's abstinence, to bring the transference into bold profile.

Approaching the position of the psychoanalyst from a structural point of view, Anna Freud (1954) placed emphasis on the psychoanalyst's maintaining an equal distance from the three agencies of the mind—ego, superego, and id. Her spatial metaphor is useful and convincing as the psychoanalyst is drawn to or repulsed by the patient's drives, wishes, and other psychological imperatives; the patient's need for various constraints, including guilt and fear of loss of love; and the patient's inability to evaluate eventualities and consequences. In Anna Freud's description, the psychoanalyst attempts to identify while avoiding becoming a party to the demands of or the deficiencies in the patient's psychodynamics, while at the same time maintaining a warm, empathic, responsive understanding. As clinically useful as Anna Freud's description is, it adds little to our understanding of what is psychodynamically required of the psychotherapist.

Gill (1954), in a discussion of the psychoanalyst in the interaction, made neutrality adjectival: "Psychoanalysis is that technique . . . employed by a *neutral analyst.* . . . [The psychoanalyst] always remains neutral in the basic sense of never trying to mold the patient in his own image" (pp. 775–776, italics added). Gill essentially restated Freud's (1919) admonition, "We refuse most emphatically to turn a patient into our private property, to decide his fate for him, to force our own ideals upon him, and with the pride of a Creator to form him in our own image [and to] affect his individuality" (p. 164).

The idea of the neutral psychoanalyst is easily misunderstood. It is clear that the neutral stance is not to be translated as one of coolness, aloofness, or niggardliness. Even Karl Menninger (1936), although entertaining the possibility that a psychoanalysis could proceed without the psychoanalyst's ever saying a word, acknowledged and illustrated the wide range of overt and covert affective, empathic, and sympathetic hidden and revealed responses of the psychoanalyst during the course of a psychoanalysis.

Neutrality is not lack of emotional involvement; what seem measured responses are manifestations of the psychoanalyst's assiduous attempt to conduct the exchange with minimal distortion created by the psychoanalyst's expectations and needs. This constant vigilance exemplifies psychoanalytic neutrality.

Although patients frequently complain about psychoanalytic neutrality, the psychotherapist is not *affecting* a nonresponding stance. In fact, the psychotherapist is responding fully but to a different level of meaning. For example, failure to be amused or laugh at a patient's hostile joke about psychoanalysis is not a stance or a trained stifling. The psychotherapist "reads" the exchange as covert transferential hostility. Laughing could, in this circumstance, be a collusion with the patient's covert expression of and denial of transferential hostility.

Not using the patient for one's own needs implies that the enterprise be carried on in such a way that the patient is not exploited for one's own personal, professional, or financial gain. Requests are not made of the patient. We recognize and avoid subtle gratifications, such as being flattered by being chosen by the patient or being tempted to "display" patients. The list of such possibilities is nearly limitless given the extraordinary people with whom we often are privileged to work, the degree of intimate knowledge we have about their lives, and the length of time that we are in intense association with them.

These countertransferential temptations must be identified and self-analyzed from the standpoint of the psychotherapist's personality, the meaning of the countertransference in the context of what is happening in the psychotherapist's life at the time, and, most important, in terms of the patient's capacity to induce such responses, generally and specifically. Training, experience, and ongoing self-analysis and consultation help the psychotherapist transform such complex responses from actions or temptations to "data" giving clues to the patient's central transferential response and content to transferential interpretations.

More subtle is avoiding the temptation to live vicariously the life of the patient, to possess vicariously the patient's extraordinary abilities or antisocial tendencies. It is understandable and forgivable that a patient may bore his family and friends with "My analyst said. . . ." It is pitiful when a psychotherapist can only add to conversations, "I have a patient who. . . ." The temptation of psychotherapists to flesh out their own emotionally and intellectually barren lives by living their lives through the lives of their patients was artistically articulated by Allen Wheelis (1956).

Is there a basic dynamic operating, the recognition of which helps us define neutrality beyond these ethical considerations? At a deep level, neutrality is the safeguard against the profound human tendency to make others into our own image. The tendency to perpetuate oneself in another is a strong and universal human characteristic of remarkable strength, one closely associated with fathering and the desire for immortality.

Using a different framework and lexicon, Roustang (1983) identified the tendency of the psychoanalytic situation, as an exaggeration of any interpersonal situation, to create the psychoanalyst in the patient and to create the patient in the psychoanalyst. From his sophisticated view, substantiated by his understanding of the essential affective transmission between mother and child, neutrality, while being the goal of the psychoanalyst, is an impossibility.

The human imperative I am alluding to plays on the difference between the desire to nurture (maternal desires) and the desire to guide (paternal desires). Nurturing is based on identification with; guiding is based on the desire to be identified with. Either can be altruistic or malignant, and both are highly narcissistically sustaining. Such differentiation is derived from ideas regarding the importance of the differing role of the father and the mother as persons and as concepts at varying developmental stages, particularly in preoedipal triangulations (Loewald, 1951; Mahler and Gosliner, 1955; Abelin, 1971, 1977). These ideas are not to impute a lessened importance to the desire of a psychotherapist of either sex to mother the patient, a desire that is fundamental to psychotherapy. They are intended to highlight yet another peril in the task of maintaining a psychoanalytic orientation, the desire to perpetuate oneself in another.

For the psychoanalyst, immortality is possible. The powerful psychic mechanisms of internalization, including introjection, incorporation, and identification, allow one to be carried psychically within another. Just as the Apostles discovered at the Pentecost that Christ dwelled within them after Jesus died, each of us, through the power of relationships, can be perpetuated.[6] This capacity of relationships is a powerful motivation for relating and a powerful determinant in fostering and molding the development of those entrusted to us. Such a temptation, when succumbed to in psychotherapy, both enormously enriches and at the same time severely limits the patient.

It probably is true that younger psychotherapists have more difficulty with competition with patients, with the need to be acknowledged by patients, and with jealousy of patients; older psychotherapists struggle more with the temptation to perpetuate themselves in their patients. Such countertransference problems are closely related to the place of narcissism in character development and are an essential component of object relatedness (Kohut, 1971). The governance of narcissism in the psychotherapist's psychic economy has been little discussed although it is central to any discussion of neutrality.

In actuality, neutrality is more closely tested in interactive psychotherapy than in psychoanalysis and psychoanalytically oriented psychotherapy. In psychoanalysis and psychoanalytically oriented psychotherapy, the practitioner, by keeping all the patient's direct and indirect enactment attempts at the forefront of the interpretive intervention, steadfastly resists the temptation to make the patient into his own image. The very recognition of the transference is a

---

[6]Providence provides two paths to immortality—our relationships and our work. Each can live after us. Such a view gives new meaning to Freud's definition of mental health, the capacity to love and work fully. In a sense, Freud was describing the two pathways to immortality. Psychoanalysis is as much a psychology of continuance as it is a drive psychology (Oremland, 1989).

major achievement over the psychotherapist's narcissism and temptation to make the patient into his own image.

In interactive psychotherapy, as interactions are chosen, as ways of dealing with events are presented, as behaviors are directly and indirectly modeled, and as parts and levels of interpretations are verbalized, the question becomes, what is the template that controls the selections? At best, the template is an idealized version of the psychotherapist; at worst it is the psychotherapist's self, idealized by himself. In either case, though enriching, it is restrictive.

CHAPTER 5
Phases in Psychoanalytically Oriented Psychotherapy

In teaching the technique of psychoanalysis, Freud (1913), using the metaphor of chess, noted that "the openings and end-games admit of an exhaustive systematic presentation . . ." (p. 123). He noted an initial phase and a termination phase, with the bulk of the process, the middle phase, being idiosyncratic to the dyad. Experience suggests a similar tripartite phasing in the course of psychoanalytically oriented psychotherapy. These phases are characteristic enough that when the psychoanalytically oriented psychotherapy is conducted well, even an outside observer listening to process material can usually identify the phase being presented.

Experienced practitioners generally suggest that psychoanalysis is a five- to seven-year endeavor, and this time span seems equally true of psychoanalytically oriented psychotherapy. The phases in psychoanalysis and psychoanalytically oriented psychotherapy do not distribute themselves equally; the lengths of the initial and middle phases vary tremendously. A given psychoanalysis or psychoanalytically oriented psychotherapy may have an inordinately long initial phase and a rather short middle phase or the reverse. The termination phase in psychoanalysis and psychoanalytically oriented psychotherapy tends to be of the same length, approximately nine months, regardless of the length of the first and second phases.

The linear temporal dimension of psychoanalysis and psychoanalytically oriented psychotherapy coexists with an atemporal dimension, just as the timeless unconscious underlies a time-aware conscious. Elements characteristic of the initial phase can be found throughout the course of the psychoanalytic process and reappear during periods of specific resistance, such as that accompanying an interruption. Although the material sounds like initial-phase material, when the psychotherapy is far along, the material can easily be understood in the context of what is transpiring. On interpretation by the patient or the psychotherapist, the initial-phase quality rapidly dissipates. Likewise, middle-phase qualities can appear early. The evaluation of phase is the evaluation of preponderance. The termination phase has characteristics so typical that nearly every aspect can be understood along specific dimensions.

INITIAL PHASE

Unlike the generally held view that the initial phase is characterized by conducive, inducing activities on the part of the psychotherapist in an attempt to promote a working alliance, in my opinion these activities characterize interactive rather than psychoanalytically oriented psychotherapy. In psychoanalytically oriented psychotherapy, the initial phase is characterized by identification and interpretation of the transference-resistance manifestations in multiple contexts. Unfortunately, at the beginning of psychotherapy, when little is known, the psychotherapist has to make the most significant comments and decisions. Later, when more is known, little needs to be said or decided. The psychotherapist in the initial phase weaves between the perils of incorrect and missed interpretations.

The motivation for the psychotherapy is activated not by the psychotherapist's inducement or the patient's psychological discomfort, but by the patient's developing sense of being understood and seeing things differently as resistance patterns are identified and integrated. Stated in the language of Kohut (1971, 1977, 1984), the psychotherapist's response is empathic. I, differing from Kohut, believe that what is motivating and mutative is the accuracy of the interpretation, not the feeling of being empathized with (Oremland, 1985).

A few examples from the initial phase illustrate how early the interpretive direction can be established. These examples illustrate essential differences between psychoanalytic and interactive interventions. What is said depends on many factors, including the "language" that develops between the patient and the psychotherapist and the psychotherapist's style.

A patient calls for an appointment, saying, "Dr. Jones suggested that I call you." An interpretive response is, "Is it solely his idea?" Another patient in the initial telephone contact says, "Do you have time to see me? I am not looking for anything extensive, maybe just one or two appointments." An interpretive response is, "You sound hesitant. Can we see what the problem is before we decide what we want to do?" In contrast, interactive responses vary from ignoring the content entirely and making the appointment, to a host of conducive, supportive comments. Responding interpretively in the initial telephone call illustrates how early an interpretive line can (must) be established and reminds us that nothing is "outside" the psychotherapy.

A more extensive example: During a telephone call, a patient explained that he had been referred by a psychotherapist. An appointment was made. On opening the door to the waiting room, I found a barefoot, shirtless young man with long blond hair and a flowing beard audibly chanting a mantra. Without looking up, he said, "I'll be with you in a moment." He resumed his chanting. I said, "You quickly put to test how respectful I'll be of you." Without a moment's hesitation, he gathered his clothes and went into the office and took the chair that was obviously mine. I said, "You have a way of dramatizing who's to be in charge." Smiling benignly, he said, "Which is my chair?" Thus began a psychoanalytically oriented psychotherapy that was to last for many years. This interpretive mode contrasts with interactive interventions, such as saying, "When you're ready, you may come in the office"; or the psychotherapist standing quietly until the patient acknowledges him; or the psychotherapist closing the door with the comment, "When you're ready, let me know." Such responses *use* thetransference in small power struggles in which little is made explicit.

Another example of how an interpretive line was established early in the initial hour was that of a woman who on the telephone asked for an appointment because she was depressed. She explained that she had received a major promotion in her company and was concerned that she could not "handle" it. At the first appointment, she wore a trim business suit and carried a briefcase. As her first comment while she was in the waiting room, she pointed to two keys on the table, each carrying an oversized tag marked MEN'S and WOMEN'S, and asked, "Are these the keys for the restroom?" I said, "I am struck that you begin by asking such an obvious question that makes you appear stupid." She was visibly annoyed, charged into the office without going to the restroom, and attacked me for calling her stupid. I reviewed the interchange, emphasizing that I did not call her stupid but was pointing out the way that she was relating to me.

Putting my comment aside, she talked about the difficulty she was having in assuming an important managerial position at her company. As she talked, she quickly became aware of her discomfort at being assertive and positive with men. At the end of the session, I asked if she would like to meet again. She agreed. On looking at my appointment book, I said, "May I see you Tuesday at 2:30?" She asked, "A.M. or P.M.?" She paused a moment and said, "I think I'm being stupid with you again."

In the next session, she referred to her comment about the appointment time. She became flustered, saying that she sensed a sexual meaning in her question—a 2:30 A.M. meeting? She asked if we should discuss her tendency to try to get men to do things by being "silly or flirtatious." I pointed out that she was asking for my direction to cover her own good idea. Thus began an extensive psychoanalytically oriented psychotherapy that came to a successful conclusion after four and a half years.

In the initial interview patients frequently describe their present difficulties and request leading questions. The psychotherapist can interpretively indicate that the patient is attempting to make the psychotherapist lead. Often it can be shown that the patient is wittingly or unwittingly concealing thoughts by attempting to follow the psychotherapist's ideas rather than the patient's own.

Because questions can have many meanings, the motivations for, and the implications of, the patient's questions are interpreted, not reflected back. Like making conducive comments, reflecting questions back is an interactive technique to which patients quickly "catch on," even though many respond compliantly. For example, a person who complained of chronic loneliness provided several hours of detailed history consisting largely of dates and events. At a point after a long pause, he hesitantly asked, "What do you think?" I responded, "I think you got anxious with what you were saying, realizing it was all dates and events and no people. I wonder if you didn't begin to realize that you were blocking me out—the way there are no people in what you have been telling me—and the question is to reestablish contact with me." Another patient, after giving a detailed history, impatiently asked, "Have you drawn any conclusions?" I responded, "I may have lots of thoughts, but I have an idea that if I came up with conclusions knowing so little about you, you'd have ample justification not to respect what I say."

The initial anamnesis provides an important skeleton that progressively is fleshed out over the full course of the psychotherapy, particularly in the middle phase. The fleshing out evolves not through the psychotherapist's questioning, but from the interpretation of transference resistances as the patient interweaves genetic reflections into the process. Asking questions to enlarge aspects of the anamnesis establishes an interactive pattern revealing the psychotherapist's interests and theoretical orientation and skews the development of the psychoanalytic process.

No attempt is made to "keep the patient talking," a technique that reflects the erroneous view that catharsis and putting thoughts into words have a primary psychotherapeutic function. The patient's free-associative flow is the result of the accurate identification of resistance processes.

Exemplifying the difficulties of establishing an interpretive line was an unemployed teacher who was referred by her child's psychotherapist. In the first session she appeared stilted, artificially composed, self-depreciating, and reeking of strong perfume. At the second session a few days later, I barely recognized her. Her face was swollen, and her appearance markedly dilapidated. She had been on an alcoholic binge. Clearly, her excessive drinking covered a severe borderline personality organization. Several times in the past she had been hospitalized for excessive drinking, suicide attempts, slashing herself, and psychotic regression. She was again on the brink of hospitalization.

I arranged to see her daily because of her extreme anxiety and fragile object constancy. In between appointments she called an incredible number of times. Over an hour, there might be 15 to 20 calls on the answering machine, mostly hang-ups. I was reasonably sure it was she who had called. Referring to the telephone contacts, which were frequent, I told her that she had lost a sense of my being there and felt panicky and disorganized. I told her that the hang-ups reflected the way she felt, that there was no she, that she felt as "empty as a hang-up." After my interpretation, she frequently left the message, "I just wanted to hear your voice," and the telephone calls markedly decreased.

The sessions continued to be extraordinarily difficult. She was frequently intoxicated. Wild screaming alternated with massive sobbing, incessant threats to slash herself and commit suicide, and despairing threats to get drunk. She pleaded with me to send her to the hospital, where she could sleep, perpetually anesthetized by medication. She wanted to blank out her mind. I repeatedly indicated that she feared to think. I added that she feared that I could not be relied upon and that she was afraid to count on me.

Her condition deteriorated. She insisted that I throw her out. I told her that she was provoking my doing what she feared I wanted to do. I elaborated that the drinking, threats of going to the hospital, slashing, and suicide were "your way of saying that you cannot be with me because you fear I cannot be relied upon, that I will disappoint you, leave you, or even disappear." I frequently added, "You say I don't want to be with you. In fact, you can't be with me. Your coming to the sessions drunk is your way of saying that you can't be with me; drinking after the sessions is your erasing what I said. Both are intended to make me not want to continue with you." She took my saying "You can't be with me and you want to make me not want to continue with you" to mean that if she did not stop drinking I would not see her. She insisted that I was giving her an ultimatum. I pointed out that she made it seem so. Suddenly, she stopped drinking, an abstinence that continued.

Despite my frequent correction of her idea of "the ultimatum," she told her accountant husband, friends, parents, and her child's psychotherapist that I had given her an ultimatum that if she did not stop drinking I would not see her and that was why she had stopped drinking. They expressed relief that at last I had "taken a strong stand and was no longer being manipulated by her." It became a treasured secret of hers that she had stopped drinking because of what I said, not because of a threat.

She began teasing me playfully about "your ultimatum." It was not until we were well into the middle phase, a year and a half later, that the intensity of her abandonment fears, centering on her erratic, alcoholic, psychotic mother, were directly expressed. Gradually we could see that her acting "crazy" with me was to make me throw her out the way she wished her lawyer father had thrown out her mother. Pretending that I had given her an ultimatum was an enactment of what she had wished her father had done with her mother. The insidious malignancy of her fear of disappointment did not fully reveal itself until we began to identify her father's bitter, self-centered paranoia.

THE MIDDLE PHASE

The middle phase of psychoanalytically oriented psychotherapy is characterized by extensive reworking of the material developed through interpretation of enactments in the transference during the initial phase. Although interpretation of transference enactments in the initial phase frequently leads to memories of past experiences and a fleshing out of the anamnesis, such recollections and discoveries of a variety of repressed and otherwise defended against historical material increase in fullness and become progressively integrated during the middle phase. The transference at this point largely provides a protective aegis under which forbidden and frightening thoughts come to the fore. More impressive are the everyday interactions that become the vehicle, so to speak, for further working through of the large variety of transferentially determined ways of reacting and behaving.

The relationships with spouse, children, siblings, colleagues, and superiors become areas of primary evaluation. Heightened understanding comes from recognition of transference-related personality characteristics and remembrances of sectors of past experience. Transference takes on its fullest and broadest meaning.

New ways of dealing with people emerge, and new experiences are sought. Conscious attempts to correct old patterns coincide with desires to revisit places and people important in the past. Although presented as part of a reassessment of the past, such desires and visits often are last-ditch attempts to change the past. The psychotherapist initially is frequently unsuccessful in reminding the patient that psychotherapy does not change the past or make people behave differently toward the patient, that psychotherapy largely helps the patient see the past and the present differently—to be different.

The patient's trying out new ways of behaving presents challenging decisions for the psychotherapist. It is difficult to determine whether a proposed view or a new activity is an attempt to circumvent aspects of the psychotherapy or is progressive movement toward change as the result of the psychotherapy. Most often the new view or activity is both. Even though the moves are "positive," what is being circumvented must be ferreted out. Unlike initial-phase material, in which confrontation is necessary to obviate action in the service of furthering the development of material within a transference context, in the middle phase, preconscious representations are more available; and interpretations by the patient and the psychotherapist are easily and accurately formulated, with new ideas readily added.

The psychotherapist, through increased knowledge of the patient's personality and personal history, is able to help the patient evaluate present relationships and bring developmental perspectives to what the patient presents. These *extratransferential* clarifications and interpretations, an attempt to provide new perspectives and enhance working through, are offered cautiously.

Often extratransference interpretations are experienced by the patient as an alliance between the psychotherapist and the patient against a particular person or circumstance. Great care must be taken to identify the transferential elaboration that is being placed on the psychotherapist's ideas. Failure can result in critical, at times destructive, acting out that is seemingly condoned by the psychotherapist.

The middle phase is generally experienced by both psychotherapist and patient as conducive, productive, and evolving. This "positive" quality requires scrutiny to be certain that transferential gratifications coexist with, but do not replace, life-enhancing experience. It is easy for the psychotherapy to stagnate into an endless, acted-out, "positive" transference. Care must be exercised that a subtle, repeating, "regressive" mode does not underlie the conducive progress.

Because of a quality of evolution from what has gone before, middle-phase work does not lend itself well to illustration and offers less dramatic case illustrations than does first-phase work. The richness of the material, especially the vitality of the interplay, quickly flattens as it is described. Despite the contrived quality that may appear to creep in, I return to a few of the cases discussed earlier.

The hippie meditator, after a period of profound depression in which a great deal of work was done on self-hate, fear of competitive interactions, and transference idealizations made a physical transformation. We had been working for months on the significance of his appearance as his proclamation that he was not controlled by society's (parental/transference) demands when one day he appeared at his appointment clean shaven, with a stylish haircut, and wearing a necktie and a tweed coat. He enjoyed the fact that I did not recognize him. "My transfiguration," he called it and shyly disclosed that he was rematriculating at the university. Slowly he revealed his inordinate, paranoid fears of competition. His projected, competitive hostility made fellow students into jeering monsters. He endowed professors, particularly male professors, with sarcasm and scheming sadistic desires. All told, the university was a terrifying place, a place where there was no one to whom to turn.

As his fears were considered in relation to his chronically ill, bitter, sarcastic father and his intrusive, incessantly questioning mother, he was able to reenter the university. It was fascinating to see him toy with the idea of becoming a psychologist. As we discussed this interest in the context of the transference, we could see his needing and fearing being lesser than I. He saw being a psychologist as lesser than being a psychiatrist; at the same time, to torment me, he saw being a psychiatrist as lesser than being a psychologist; in effect, he wanted to be me. After several psychology courses, he lost interest in psychology and eventually received an M.B.A. It was easy to see that he was emulating, and even exceeding, his father, a successful businessman. His finding his vocation (identity) puts in vivid profile the importance of transference interpretation, including interpretation of the "positive" transference, in enabling a patient to make selections based on insightful rather than enactment dynamics.

For the borderline teacher with periodic bouts of drinking, the middle phase was slow to come. The intense, demanding, formless "help me" with which she bombarded me gradually gave way to relating the severity of her mother's psychotic behavior and her own fears of having no one. In the background was her reluctance to recognize the intensity of her anger toward her father for not intervening and for leaving her alone psychologically as well as physically with the erratic, vicious mother.

As she talked about having "no one," I suggested that "no one" meant "parents." By her incessant desire to make everyone, including her children, into parents, she drove everyone away. The intensity of her demandingness can hardly be overstated. We talked about the essence of being a mother—taking onto oneself whatever is necessary to protect the child. I indicated that by not being a good parent to her children, she was repeating what she had experienced. She shuddered with despair as she realized what she had done and was doing to her children. She was flooded with regrets. Her list was long, tragic and dismaying—a daughter psychotically anorectic, a son deeply depressed, and another son continually in trouble with the law. It was a family in chaos.

In response to wailing requests that I eradicate her bad memories, I pointed out that bad memories could be mitigated only by placing them into perspective, that bad memories cannot be eradicated but can be counteracted by good memories. Her pleas for help resulted in her bringing to the sessions highly detailed descriptions of the difficult circumstances in her children's lives. As we reviewed the children's manifold problems, we could see that she was attempting to develop a new way of being and relating, and her family began to flourish.

For example, when she was bitterly bemoaning car pooling and having to wait for the children, I pointed out, "Do you ever go into the school to get them?" She panicked. Looking carefully, we could see that she was fearful of seeing her children's teachers because they knew what a "drunk" she had been and what a "mess" her children were. I pointed out that she was placing her bad feelings about herself onto others and was becoming afraid of them. She then told me of the dreadful, jeering voices that "are in my head."

We discussed that she kept the bad part of mothering (the car pooling) for herself and did not allow herself to participate in the good part (watching the children develop). Subsequently, she went into the children's school instead of waiting impatiently outside. She was astonished at the response. Her children introduced her to their friends, giving her a new view of their lives and abilities. She could see that they were not the avaricious monsters that she saw them as being. We began to discuss her projecting her devouring dependency feelings onto the children. The teachers told her of the noticeable improvement in the children, and everyone commented on how much better she looked. It was clear that being better produced good things—that being a good parent could produce good thoughts. She began to cook for her children rather than order in food, mostly pizza, as she had done for more years than she could remember.

The stories of her attempts to mother her children and their responses are among the most poignant moments I can remember of any psychotherapy. She wept profusely, and I was wet eyed myself as she related how one day her 13-year-old daughter came into her bedroom and said, "Mom, I was just thinking of all you do for us. You found my talking doctor for me. You drive me to him four times a week. You found our tutors and drive us to them. You cook wonderful food for us. You help us with our homework, and you give the best hugs in the world."

After the cessation of her drinking and her remarkable reorganization of her life, her husband told her that he wanted a divorce. Evidently he had waited until she was strong enough so that he could leave.

The divorce introduced a host of new anxieties. Being dependent on her ex-husband's espousal and child support, she worried incessantly about running out of money. (Her financially well-off parents early on definitively and cruelly had told her that she could not look to them in any way for financial support.)

Although she received a generous divorce settlement, the high cost of psychotherapy for her and her daughter and the extensive tutoring that her children needed required her to use money from savings each month. She had severe panic attacks, with vivid images of being a street person and "homeless." She always had difficulty with "spending too much" and "buying everything she wanted." In discussing the fear of running out of money, we looked carefully at her spending. Although there was an impulsive quality to the way she bought things, in fact, most of what she bought were essentials. She had incorporated her mother's and her husband's accusations. "You have no sense. You buy everything in sight. You are a sucker for any salesperson. You will be in the poor house before you are 40." became self-concepts that easily became jeering voices.

Despite work on her fears of "running out of money," the panic attacks about finances were unrelenting. One day while discussing her high gasoline bills incurred because of the extensive commuting for her and her daughter's frequent psychotherapy, tutors, and car pools, I realized that she bought gasoline at full-service gasoline stations.[1] I asked her about the service stations. She became agitated, insisting that it was unimportant. Hysterically stamping her feet, she cried out, "I'll never use self-service gas. You can't make me." I pointed out the intensity of the "never" and the "you can't make me," a reaction that previously had been identified as an internalization of her mother's characteristic response to requests. In the next sessions, we could see her extraordinary fears of self-service gasoline stations—that the hose would become uncontrollable, that the gas would flood out of the tank, and that there would be a spark and everything would explode. We talked, as we had many times before, about the catastrophic quality to her fears.

After many months she tried a self-service station. The hose kinked and gasoline splashed around. The service station owner ran to her. She became terrified that he would "bawl her out." Rather than berating her, he told her, to her astonishment, that he was extremely sorry for what happened and offered to have her car washed and her clothes cleaned. Instead of being comforted, she sobbed hysterically that she could never do anything right.

We discussed the incident extensively. She accused me of getting her "into that mess." After a month, she cautiously approached the

---

[1]Frequently in middle phase work, an insignificant issue can be telling. In some ways the insignificance of the issue puts difficult-to-acknowledge factors in bold relief.

same self-service station again. The owner recognized her and came over to help. She thanked him and said, "I want to try it myself." Under his careful eye, the filling went smoothly. She was delighted to learn that she had saved over $2.00. We talked about how her fears kept her dependent and vulnerable and contributed to the feeling that she had no control over anything, including her money.

The effect of this discussion quickly spread to other fears—of supermarkets, anything electrical, machines of all sorts, and work around the swimming pool. Having discovered that she could save money, that she was gaining mastery and ability, she gained self-confidence, self-esteem, independence, and a strong sense that the "stream out" (the money) was being stemmed.

The woman with the restroom keys had a relatively short middle phase that was marked by a rapid increase in self-confidence and inner serenity. Notable was her meteoric rise at work, which was facilitated by the fact that companies were looking for qualified, experienced women for high-level managerial positions. The middle phase was characterized by relatively little genetic reconstruction, although it was clear that when she spent time with her family, the relationships were easier. She asked family members many questions, and they had discussions of a "depth that we never had before."

The middle-phase material largely concerned developments at work, her growing ability to work with and lead men, and her unsatisfactory male relationships outside work. Sadly, she recognized that her relationships outside work were not going to improve. Her physical appearance, increasing age, and high-level work position made it hard to find suitable men. Younger men were not interested in her except as a "mother" or as "income." Older men who were interested in her were generally passive or boring. She deplored the fact that her male cohorts could date and marry women from a broader range of ages and professional experience than the men she could consider. She realized that envy of men and their "easy" situation did not help her. She began constructing a life as a single woman, regretfully resigning herself to not having a family of her own.[2]

---

[2]She returned five years after completing her psychotherapy, as she approached

THE TERMINATION PHASE

A great deal has been written about the criteria for and the process of termination of psychoanalysis (Jones, 1948; Balint, 1950; Bridger, 1950; Hoffer, 1950; Klein, 1950; Firestein, 1974). Because psychotherapy is largely regarded as symptom oriented, criteria for termination are little discussed and generally related to the fate of the presenting difficulties. Yet, in practice, the psychotherapies, like psychoanalyses, tend to be extensive endeavors to change character.

In a parallel fashion, the termination process of psychotherapy, unlike the termination process of psychoanalysis, has been largely neglected. A wide range of views exists regarding the process of terminating psychotherapy, and the process is determined by the patient more than is generally acknowledged. Most terminations in psychotherapy are viewed interactively as variants of a weaning process.

In contrast, in properly conducted psychoanalytically oriented psychotherapy, just as in psychoanalysis, the presenting symptoms are usually resolved early in the psychotherapy. The greater aim, the "after-education," becomes an unspoken goal. The criteria for termination in psychoanalytically oriented psychotherapy follow closely those for psychoanalysis. Yet in both psychoanalytically oriented psychotherapy and psychoanalysis most criteria for symptom and character change are not fundamental to the decision to terminate. Most psychoanalysts determine termination by evaluating where the patient is in the process of the psychoanalysis rather than by clinical phenomena. I propose that the situation is identical for psychoanalytically oriented psychotherapy.

In the middle phase of psychoanalytically oriented psychotherapy, freely associating, that is, speaking freely and fully about material in the multiple contexts of past, present, and transference, predominates but is more tied to events and actualities of the

---

age 40, saying that she wanted to consider having a child although unmarried. After extensive discussion, she decided that she was ready and asked if I would see her in "supportive psychotherapy" while she explored the possibilities. I saw her "interactively," by my criteria, until a month prior to the birth of her son. Since that time, I see her periodically. I admire her skill as a mother, skillful and organized homemaker, and highly paid executive.

transference than in psychoanalysis. This freeness in thinking and speaking is an achievement of the middle phase and a major indicator that termination can be considered (Buxbaum, 1950; Glover, 1955; Oremland, 1973). The psychotherapist adds little, not because of being excluded but because the patient's material is widely inclusive. There is a synergistic quality as each adds to the other's thoughts. The myriad of protestations, requests, and demands to stop the sessions are in the past. As it becomes increasingly clear that the process (looking together) is endless, it also becomes clear that the procedure (the psychotherapy) need not be. The decision to terminate does not arise out of a sense that thematically there is little more to work on; rather, initiating termination is part of the consistent sense that a mutual *mode* of working has been achieved. Stated simply, termination in psychoanalytically oriented psychotherapy is not the result of a "petering out" or a "plateauing"; rather, termination is inextricably part of the heightened, consistent sense of synergistically discovering together.

The process of termination, like the process of initiating and continuing psychotherapy, is the result of the psychotherapist's interpretive work. Francois Roustang (1983) underlined this fact in a poetical way. Referring to Freud's pathetic attempts to terminate an apparently interminable psychoanalysis by interactive means, an invitation to dinner, Roustang noted,

> although there should no longer be an analyst at the end of analysis [the analyst can become] something much worse, the analyst with a capital A. Invitations to dinner . . . do not lead to the dissolution of [the transference], they are ways of embalming [the analyst] and of building a mausoleum for him [p. 62].

Termination is an active process that is sustained by the psychotherapist's interpretation of the patient's responses to the impending separation from, and loss of, the psychotherapist and the psychotherapy. In short, termination is an interpretively guided, insight-enhancing process that is closely related to response to loss and mourning (Fenichel, 1924; Buxbaum, 1950; Hoffer, 1950; Weigert, 1952; Oremland, 1973).

At some point the patient or psychotherapist raises the issue of possibly finishing. Thoughts of termination are strikingly alive in the minds of both psychotherapist and patient. These thoughts are often associated with preconscious representations and fantasies about the relationship when the psychotherapy is completed, and often there are direct expressions of appreciation for what has been accomplished. The words the patient chooses reflect in an uncontrived way a quality of ending or completing. They are free of any quitting or stopping, resistance manifestations. The appreciation is deeply gratifying to and is easily accepted by the psychotherapist because of mode and content. It is realistic, well documented, and stands in marked contrast to the idealizations that defended against anger, competitive conflicts, and attempts not to deal with disappointing objects.

After discussion, the psychotherapist agrees to the idea of completing. Regardless of how interpretive the psychoanalytically oriented psychotherapy has been, the psychotherapist's saying "I think we can begin to think about finishing" is a major interactive comment, the second major interactive comment of the psychotherapy. Its significance and repercussions are second only to the first major interactive comment of the psychotherapy, "I think we should meet regularly."

As with any impending loss, on presentation and confirmation of the idea of finishing, the patient experiences disbelief, sadness, joy, and uncertainty. After a number of months, as these feelings are interpreted in terms of separation and loss, a date for ending is established; this is the third major interaction in the psychotherapy. With surprising frequency the presenting or primary symptom recurs. In termination, the primary symptom, as Ernest Jones (1948) stated, "[attains] almost mystical significance" as a representation of the patient's desire to begin again—a defense against the loss of the transference-endowed figure.

The recrudescence of the primary symptom requires reworking of the major material of the psychotherapy in relation to impending separation and loss. Incidents of the psychotherapy, intermixed with remembrances of forgotten and previously considered abandonments, appear during and outside the sessions as vivid, bittersweet, at times painful, unbidden, poignant reveries. Like the reveries of mourning, these remembrances, when fully appraised, effect a further working through. Often this working through is combined with fantasy explorations about the posttherapeutic relationship. The fantasies are transferential expressions and attempts to experiment with new ways of relating to the psychotherapist, both as a person and as a prototype. As one patient said, "Is there an Oremland Alumni Club?"

In 1973, I described a specific dream that frequently occurs during the termination phase of successful psychoanalysis. It also occurs with regularity during termination work in successful psychoanalytically oriented psychotherapy. In the dream, the psychotherapist appears as himself or herself, usually in relation to the presenting symptom, which often shows modification. The timing of the occurrence of the dream is symbolic, for the dream usually occurs shortly after termination is confirmed, shortly after a termination date is established, the night before the first appointment of the last week of the psychotherapy, or the night before the last appointment. The psychotherapist's appearing as himself or herself is a manifest element representing the latent recognition of the work done on the transference distortions. The modification of the primary symptom is a manifest element representing the latent recognition of the work done on the pathology.

These specific termination phenomena—the recrudescence of the primary symptom; the reworking of the material of the psychotherapy in relation to separation and loss; unbidden, vivid reveries of various incidents of the psychotherapy that emerge with the reworking of the material; and, less consistently, the specific termination dream—are strong indications that the psychotherapy has altered the character of the patient and represents more than just a helpful relationship. In short, these phenomena affirm that a psychoanalytic process was initiated, has been worked through, and is concluding (Jones, 1948; Buxbaum, 1950; Glover, 1955; Oremland, 1973). They are nonexistent in psychotherapies aborted by patients, although the phenomena, except the specific termination dream may occur with great intensity in psychotherapies aborted by psychotherapists. Further, such phenomena are distinctly muted in the termination of interactive psychotherapies because of the typical "weaning" and deintensifying interventions designed to produce identificatory-incorporative, rather than insight-producing, gains.

With regard to the psychotherapist's countertransference, the parallel uncertainties of termination intermixed with the defenses against loss are experienced in various ways. Often the defense against loss is experienced as concern about incompleteness of the work. Sometimes the defense against loss is experienced by the psychotherapist as concern about open hours, a derivative expression of how irreplaceable the patient is. At times there is the convoluted concern that the patient is being terminated prematurely because the psychotherapist is afraid that he or she is holding on to the patient because of fear of empty hours. In short, a host of concerns may be expressions of fears of being left bereft.

The recrudescence of the primary symptom presents special problems. As Jones (1948) commented, "In my experiences, [the primary symptom] has mostly been the last symptom to disappear . . . being taken as a battle-ground between patient and analyst, a test-case of the fight between the resistance and the analysis" (p. 381). This "battle over the presenting symptom" imbues the termination with an uneasy quality as the psychotherapist struggles to decide, sometimes up to the last hour, if this is a termination recrudescence of the primary symptom or if the symptom had fallen from being actively reported, the psychotherapy is incomplete, and the termination needs to be renegotiated.

Paradoxically, the final hour often is anticlimactic, marked by awkwardness. It is something like seeing a friend off at the airport and learning that departure of the airplane has been delayed. You are together after the last good-bye. Yet as the hour ends and there is a parting handshake, often there is a rush of poignant feelings, and often, I am told, even a not-too-well-held-back tear on both sides.

The mourning process of the termination phase continues after the psychotherapy has concluded as the psychotherapist and the psychotherapy are decathected and integrated with concomitant solidification of gains. For both patient and psychotherapist, the period following the last hour is characterized by doubt, exhilaration, sadness, and vivid reveries of various events of the psychotherapy as the mourning continues. Particularly, the unrealized expectations of the psychotherapy are worked through repeatedly with an increasingly realistic appraisal of what has been accomplished.

Later, contact may occur because of the professional inbreeding of the psychotherapy field or because of a chance meeting at an event of mutual interest. Always there is special feeling in that aspects of the transference and countertransference, although analyzed, are easily reactivated (Oremland, Blacker, and Norman, 1975; Norman et al., 1976). After all, one always remains the other's psychotherapist or patient. A friendship may develop, and sometimes regretfully both psychotherapist and former patient discover that they do not like each other that much.

Often the only subsequent contact is a call in a time of crisis or when the patient needs advice. For the most part, though, former patients disappear from our lives, or we only receive a card at Christmas, when the repression barrier on expressing feelings to important people from one's past is diminished. More often than we might like, the next time we hear about even a successfully terminated patient is when a colleague says that the patient has resumed psychotherapy.

In summary, in psychoanalytically oriented psychotherapy, as in psychoanalysis, there are phase-specific predominances that characterize the progressions culminating in a termination with identifiable specifics. Termination in each is the result of an active interpretive process at base akin to mourning. Termination is a mourning on both sides for the psychotherapist and the patient have been friends and companions on a unique journey, a journey remarkably heightened by transference–countertransference imperatives. An important part of the final stages of this mourning process for both psychotherapist and patient is the mourning of unfulfilled goals of the psychotherapy, many of which were themselves unrealistic transference and countertransference expectations.

Typical of psychoanalytically oriented psychotherapy, during each phase, the "working through," which solidifies insight, is accomplished through the interpretation of the derivative transference-based material presented by the patient. At every phase, the psychotherapist is the *silent* beneficiary of new integrations as the patient's psychotherapy progresses.

CHAPTER 6

The Dream in Psychoanalytically Oriented Psychotherapy

Dreams have an exceptional position in the history of psychoanalysis as a theory, a technique, and a social movement. Dreams played a significant role in Freud's psychoanalytic self-observation, and the publication of the *Interpretation of Dreams* (Freud, 1900) was the first major public exposition of his theories and technique. The *Interpretation of Dreams* gathered to Freud his most important and talented early students, Sandor Ferenczi, Ernest Jones, and Carl Jung.

The place of dreams and dreaming in the *theory* of psychoanalysis is exceptional. Investigation of dreams has produced such important concepts as primary and secondary process, condensation, displacement, transference, the self-observing functioning of the ego, and means of representation. Dreams provide a nonpathological opportunity to study psychophysiological interplay.

The primacy of dreams in the *technique* of psychoanalysis is controversial. Central to the controversy is whether dream material in clinical work is of exceptional importance deserving special detailed attention, or whether dream material is an element of a session and, like any other element, is dealt with as the session unfolds (Waldhorn, 1967; Greenson, 1970). Less clearly articulated in the controversy is the interactive significance of affording a dream, or selective elements of a dream, specific attention.

Like other aspects of the psychotherapeutic interplay, the difference between the place of dreams in interactive psychotherapy and in psychoanalytically oriented psychotherapy and psychoanalysis is more marked than the difference between the place of dreams in psychoanalytically oriented psychotherapy and in psychoanalysis. In interactive psychotherapy, the psychotherapist selects the dream in totality, elements of the dream, or aspects of the reporting of dreams to illustrate specific concerns or to emphasize or imply specific directions of thinking or acting. In keeping with the therapeutic orientation, the dream in its totality or any of its elements, like any aspect of the interplay, is used to achieve therapeutic goals explicitly or implicitly defined by the psychotherapist and the patient. Often confirmatory "messages" are read into the dream narrative taken in its totality: "I guess the dream tells us that you are now ready for . . ."

Although choice of elements is obviously interactive in that selection directs emphasis, paradoxically Erikson's (1954) "exhaustive study," the classical element-by-element approach, also has a strong interactive effect. Erikson's exhaustive study easily leads to unrecognized and unanalyzed, exquisite, transferentially elaborated, empathic mutualities as psychoanalyst and patient, in session after session, find ever more wonderous meanings in the patient's ephemeral production. Nonetheless, the exhaustive study contrasts in subtle ways with interactive psychotherapy. In the exhaustive study the dream is fully explored in the interest of increasing the patient's self-awareness, an aftereducation, not for specific therapeutic gains.

There is an affinity among the topographical model of psychoanalytic metapsychology, the view that dreams are exceptional clinical material, and the technical approach of isolating dream elements for association (Freud, 1900; Erikson, 1954; Waldhorn, 1967). Even though there is currently controversy in psychoanalysis about the element-by-element technique, it is used more frequently than is generally realized. "How about the . . . ?", "What do you think about the . . . ?"—interventions referring to an element of a dream when there is a resistive interruption in the associative flow or when there is lack of attention to the dream or an element of it are common even among psychoanalysts who condemn the "exceptional view" (see, for example, the case process reports in the Waldhorn, 1967, monograph).

The view of dreams as part of the ongoing associative flow of a session, a process approach, has an affinity to the structural model of psychoanalytic metapsychology, an emphasis on the analysis of resistance, and psychoanalytically oriented psychotherapy as well as psychoanalysis. In the process approach, all elements of the patient's material are regarded as reflecting multidetermined imperatives and as potentially equally revealing (Erikson, 1954; Waldhorn, 1967; Greenson, 1970). This view translates technically into dealing with the dream as part of a process in which resistances, including resistance to thinking about a dream in totality or in part, are identified and interpreted. The interpretations remain equally involved with all the material so as to increase awareness of all aspects of the interplay. The guiding central organizer of the interpretations is the transference as the dream makes visible, and the associations to it vividly confirm and anticipate, the transference.

Rudiments of the process approach can be found in the *Interpretation of Dreams,* in which Freud (1900) identified the small asides and incidental labels applied to dreams as the *gloss* in dreams. Freud recognized that such comments about the dream, as "I had a strange dream last night," "I had a crazy dream," or "I remember only part of a dream" were attempts to disguise the dream or render it meaningless.

The gloss and comments more directly involving the psychotherapist, such as "Are you interested in dreams?" and "In that this is analysis [even when it is not], I guess I should tell you my dreams," are essentially highly transferential associations to the dream. Such comments can be interpreted as transferential fear of ridicule, of being irrational, or of competitive conflicts. The patient is aware of the imbalance of knowledge, and the psychotherapist is seen as having the upper hand (Oremland, 1978).

The earliest clear recognition of a broader communicative function in dreaming was Ferenczi's (1913a) paper, "To Whom Does One Relate One's Dreams?" Ferenczi early remarked that a dream may be dreamed as much for someone else as it is for other reasons.[1] In this communicative context, the reported dream is best seen as

---

[1]Freud (1900) recognized that some people, not just patients, dreamed dreams and told him their dreams to prove his theories incorrect—an early recognition of transference.

the first transferential elaboration, a step beyond secondary revision (Brenner, cited in Waldhorn, 1967; Breznitz, 1971; Silber, 1973).

If there is validity to the view that dreams hold an exceptional place in the technique of psychoanalysis, psychoanalytically oriented psychotherapy has not been burdened by a parallel controversy. Because psychoanalytically oriented psychotherapy focuses on the actualities of the interaction to identify transferential patterns, every aspect of the dream, like any material of a session, its presentation, and its content, is considered in the context of how, when, and why it is reported. The focus on context includes an acute awareness of resistance manifested in dreaming, the long dream, the overly detailed dream, the dream fragment, and dreaming about something so as not to talk about it. In short, all the resistance patterns regarding dreaming and dreams that characterize psychoanalysis apply to psychoanalytically oriented psychotherapy. Yet as in other aspects of the psychotherapeutic interplay, the meanings of the dream in psychoanalytically oriented psychotherapy tend to unfold within a stronger interpersonal (transferential) context than in psychoanalysis.[2]

For example, a stockbroker complained of anxiety and fear of failure. A tense young man who spoke rapidly, with characteristic impatience, he ended my sentences and corrected whatever I said. Often he substituted synonyms for my words as though his choices were more apt than mine. His dream was part of a series of intense sessions discussing his competitiveness with me.

"I had a dream last night, *really interesting.* You know, yesterday I bought a Swiss Army knife. It was not the most elaborate kind. I would have liked one of those, but they were too big and heavy. In the dream I put the knife in my pants pocket. As I was walking down the street, the knife slipped down my pant leg and came out the cuff. It was really strange. It was in my pocket but stretched down further and further until it showed. Well, that was the dream."

There was a short pause, and then he said, "I wonder what I

---

[2]This discussion is not intended to detail the multiple manifestations and ramifications of the analysis of dreams and dreaming in psychoanalytically oriented psychotherapy. Rather the discussion essentially illustrates the place of the dream in psychoanalytically oriented psychotherapy and indicates the similarities to and the differences from interactive psychotherapy and psychoanalysis.

would have dreamed if I hadn't bought the knife?" I pointed out that he was "inviting us to go into the never-never land of supposition." He talked about the uncomfortable feeling he had when he thought I had the advantage. "If I take us into areas of supposition, then we're both guessing." After a short pause, he said, "I was afraid that you would interpret the dream as phallic exhibitionism. I thought to myself I couldn't stand it if he does. It would be so trite, so textbookish."

I pointed out his fear of his contempt of me. "When I fail you, it makes you anxious because you fear you'll lay into me." I added, "Even though an idea is trite, it doesn't mean it is incorrect." He agreed that the content of the dream was "of interest" and again talked about how relieved he was that I had not said "the obvious." He reviewed many incidents in which "it was all that I could do to keep from expressing complete disgust at your obviousness. It was all I could do to keep from saying, 'Is that all you have to offer?' " I pointed out that even saying that the dream was "really interesting" was to call my attention to the importance of the dream, to keep me from missing something—that he was instructing me, in a sense to strengthen me, to protect me from his contempt. He sensed a paradox. He feared that the dream was of great significance and that the "great bungler will miss it" and he would feel utter contempt and, at the same time, that the dream was insignificant and that I would "sneer" at it. As the sessions continued he explored the extent and the fear of his contempt and how frequently he felt that I was impeding the progress of his psychotherapy.[3]

Dreams from the past and recurrent dreams are explored primarily transferentially to reveal the relation of talking about or relating the dream to the current moment in the psychotherapy. For exam-

---

[3]After over two years of psychoanalytically oriented psychotherapy and with increasing insight into his competitive struggles with me, he considered increasing the frequency and using the couch. Wryly, he called this a "Pyrrhic victory," which began the discussion, that continued in the psychoanalysis, of what he and I both had to lose in order to be together. In retrospect, I do not feel that there was much difference in the level of material or the areas of exploration in the psychoanalysis as compared with the psychoanalytically oriented psychotherapy. It seemed more like a psychoanalytically oriented psychotherapy four times a week on the couch. Eventually, we came to a mutual decision to terminate after six years and much evident improvement.

ple, a 27-year-old man, unusually attractive and winning in his manner, was referred for depression, that severely interfered with his work. He explained that he was recently divorced, "I just can't adjust to the divorce. I am extremely remorseful."

He continued, "At the university I was the student body president and she, the vice-president; I, a star athlete and she, a cheerleader. It seemed natural that we should marry. Our families were heavily involved. Each family accurately saw the other family as influential, wealthy, and well placed. The marriage was widely regarded as a good match—a marriage of dynasties. There was one problem—we didn't really like each other that much. I think we fulfilled everyone else's fantasies."

After several years of marriage, he was suspicious that his wife was seeing a friend of his. He asked her, and she complained about his possessiveness. A short time later he found them together, making love. Nonetheless, they reassessed their marriage and decided to devote themselves to it once again. After a short time, he again became suspicious. When he confronted her, she acknowledged her infidelity, told him that their life was boring, and asked for a divorce.

Early in the psychotherapy, while talking about his intense remorse, I said that the divorce seemed "more a blow to your pride than a loss." He responded, "It was a great embarrassment. I had never failed at anything before." He placed his head in his hands, sobbed quietly, and murmured, "What an empty person I am." I pointed out, "You can't face me with thoughts like that."

In the next session, he talked about placing his head in his hands and my comment that he couldn't face me. Suddenly he stopped and said, "I feel I ought to tell you something that is very distressing. Since early adolescence I have had a recurring dream.

"I come into my mother's bedroom, and my mother is in her dressing room. The door is open and I see that she is wearing a sheer chemise. She calls me in. As we talk, I glance away from her, and she encourages me to look at her. She says, 'You know there isn't anything a mother can't teach her son. I think the best way for you to learn about sex is for me to teach you.' At this point she slowly undresses me, we go to bed, and the dream ends."

He explained that it had always been a frequent dream. He ashamedly confessed that while masturbating, he had had since adolescence a fantasy similar to the dream. In the fantasy he was more active, asking, "Mother, won't you teach me about sex?" He explained that when he was having sexual problems with his wife, he used this fantasy to achieve potency. I responded that he was keeping his mother a part of his most intimate life.

At the next session, he told me, "This morning when I awoke I wanted to cancel the appointment. On the way to your office I realized that I had a dream last night that I didn't want to tell you. That probably is why I wanted to cancel the appointment." As he began to tell the dream, he suddenly forgot it. We talked about his fear and wish to make me a part of his intimate life, and he suddenly remembered the dream.

"It was essentially the same dream—changed. There is intercourse, and I feel all sweaty and involved. I say, 'Mother, I am going to shower.' I leave the bedroom and go into the hallway, and there is my father. I blush intensely. I know that he knows what is going on. I want to say to him, 'Can you help me?' My father looks at me. There is a sadness in his face. He seems to know that he can't help. That is where the dream ends."

In discussing the dream, he realized that there was a relation between the father's being in the dream and his having told me about the recurring dream and masturbation fantasy. I pointed out that he hoped that I could, and yet feared that I would not be able to, free him from the attachment to his mother.

It was apparent to both of us that the sequence had been initiated by my interpretation, "You can't face me with thoughts like that." More accurately, the sequence was initiated by his placing his face in his hands in an enactment of his shame and his hostile obliteration of his father for being, in his view, ineffectual. My interpretation made the enactment explicit making him literally and figuratively deal with me.[4]

Absence of thinking about a dream, like other absences, taxes the

---

[4]The psychotherapy continued for over four years with many discussions about increasing the frequency and using the couch. Although extensively analyzed, these changes never took place. During the fourth year of the psychotherapy, he remarried and about six months later was offered an attractive job in the East. After much discussion and considerable acknowledgment that the psychotherapy had been of great value, he decided to move with the intention of resuming psychotherapy and, perhaps, beginning psychoanalysis.

psychotherapist's skill. Often a comment (confrontation/interpretation) about the absence invokes associating to the dream. The transferential significance of associating to the dream in response to the intervention must be explored even though the intervention results in associating to the dream. It must be emphasized that producing associations following such an intervention does not invalidate the importance or usefulness of the material; yet, associating to the dream amounts to an acting out of the transference, frequently as compliance/defiance.

In a like fashion, a comment about the absence of dreams may produce a dream or a flood of dreams. Although the resultant dreaming has an intrinsic validity, it is a response to the intervention (interpretation/confrontation), an acting out to avoid having to consider the resistance noted, and may go unanalyzed because of its "positive" quality. At times comments on the lack of interest in dreams or the apparent absence of dreaming is the beginning of an exploration of broader characterological restrictions, including literalness related to fear of loss of control and irrationality.

In summary, in these considerations of the dream reside many of the essential differences between a psychoanalytic and an interactive orientation. It is the transferential overriding of resistance and the analysis of selective "negative" and "positive" manifestations that make a psychotherapy interactive. Psychoanalysts tend, especially with regard to dreams, not to recognize that when they override rather than analyze resistances—when they ask for thoughts about, or, worse, "associations to," specific dream elements—they are being interactive, regardless of the trappings. Their lack of recognition often reflects an overidentification with the traditional view of dreams in psychoanalysis. They fail to recognize that although dreams have an exceptional place in the history and theory of psychoanalysis, it does not follow that dreams have an exceptional place in the technique. It speaks to a general confusion in psychoanalysis regarding resistance and transference analysis, if not in theory, then at least in practice.

In some ways the discussion of dreams epitomizes the thrust of this book—that in psychoanalytically oriented psychotherapy and in psychoanalysis what practitioners do is identical—interpretation of the transference. Yet, it does not follow that even though the modes are identical, the process (the patient's material) that develops in the two modalities will be the same.

CHAPTER 7

Some Specific Interactive Situations

Some aspects of the psychotherapeutic interplay are intrinsically interactive regardless of the orientation of the psychotherapy. Dreams, fees, hours, interruptions, and the physical environment involve interactions requiring specific consideration as one attempts to establish and maintain the psychoanalytic orientation of a psychotherapy. The initiation and termination of the psychotherapy are interactions of a different order, as previously described.

FEES

Among the difficult components of psychotherapy is fee. Like many other important decisions of psychotherapy, establishing the fee comes early, when the psychotherapist has little information. It is a truism of psychotherapy that next to sex—perhaps even more than sex—the intrigues and duplicities regarding money for rich and poor are extraordinary. Without meaning and yet endowed with multiple meanings, money gives rise to richly complex attitudes.

The tendency toward a regressed, closed-system approach to subjective aspects of interpersonal relatedness (if you love them, you love me less) readily becomes evident in even the most integrated patient in regard to fees. Money becomes a reified expression of "If I give to you, I have less."

Like attitudes toward money, attitudes toward time (scheduled hours) reach a similarly regressive level of meaning when, as frequently happens, a patient loses the sense that the sessions are for him. Younger patients may see time for psychotherapy as a something taken from them. Older patients endow time with a different meaning; for them, time is something taken from them that can never be replaced. The different view of time between young and old can make psychotherapy more important to the older patient. As a woman in her 60s beginning her second analysis said, "I don't think I have the luxury this time of putting things off for my next analysis." For older psychotherapists, the feeling that something irreplaceable is being taken from them can become a difficult countertransference response to the reluctant or unresponsive patient.

Fees are established according to the patient's income, indebtedness, and style of living, as well as standards in the community. In general, psychotherapists, like society at large, charge the rich too little and the poor too much. Although they aim to be fair, psychotherapists cannot hope to correct prevailing social injustices. The matter is complicated by unconscious contributions of some people to their own low income and indebtedness.

Just as frequency is established over a period of time, the elements of the fee must be identified and interpreted systematically over time. Patients may misconstrue "taking time" in establishing fee as an attempt to "hook them." Issues regarding the relation of trust to need are played out. Yet the psychotherapist must be careful that the evaluation is not prolonged out of fear of establishing a fee.

In psychoanalytically oriented psychotherapy there is no "usual," "standard," "reduced," or "low" fee. As the various reluctances to talk about and reveal financial matters are worked through interpretively, a *fair* fee—one that is practical, reasonable, and acceptable to both patient and psychotherapist—is established.[1]

---

[1]Psychotherapy fees, like physician (becoming less so) and clergy remuneration, are perquisites rather than fees. They are evidences of compensation and are not related to the value of the service. Like the services of the clergy, for example, performing a marriage, those of a psychotherapist can be of inestimable value, or

Telling a patient that a certain fee is the psychotherapist's usual one but that (for whatever reason) the patient is being seen for a lower fee reflects countertransference and inhibits exploration of the patient's ideas about why the fee is at that level.[2]

Unstated is that fees will be increased or decreased with changing circumstances. Patients who fall on financially hard times because of emotional or external factors pose special problems. Patients who incur financial difficulties frequently make it impossible for the psychotherapy to continue. Patients may precipitate financial difficulties as a transferential test, for example, to punish the psychotherapist or to force the psychotherapist to abandon them out of fear of being abandoned by the psychotherapist.

Neither patient nor psychotherapist should see someone who he or she does not want to see. If the level of payment falls below an acceptable level for the psychotherapist, it is more respectful of the patient and more workable to refer the patient elsewhere than to continue reluctantly. On the other hand, some psychotherapists, including me, feel that patients should be seen through difficulties and their circumstances be accommodated as much as possible. Obviously sadomasochistic elements and infantile rescue fantasies must be guarded against.

Special arrangements such as splitting insurance compensation, billing the insurance company at one rate and the patient at another, carrying the patient on credit, and agreements that the low fee will be increased at a specific time contain the potential to change the psychoanalytically oriented psychotherapy into interactive work with elaborate transference–countertransference enactments that rarely can be resolved. There is little question that psychoanalytically oriented psychotherapies often fail or become endless because of enactments regarding fees, hours, and interruptions that are underanalyzed.

Insurance benefits and copayments from the family do not interfere with psychoanalytically oriented psychotherapy as long as the

---

they can be worthless. Perquisites, unlike fees, are related to circumstances rather than to the importance, need, or "market value" of the service.

[2]Psychotherapists often are afraid that their work (in fact that they) will be depreciated if the patient thinks a lower fee is the "usual fee." I have found that for most psychotherapists, "usual" is the fee they aspire to. Fee setting is a rich field for acting out by patient and psychotherapist alike.

psychotherapist deals with the patient alone and the arrangements are kept between the patient and the third party. Only minimal information has to be supplied by the psychotherapist to insurance companies, and forms completed by the psychotherapist can be given to the patients so that they deal with the third party.

Monthly statements, given to patients at the beginning of each month, offer an immediacy to the discussion of difficulties in payment. After the psychotherapy is further along, if there is no reason for a statement (e.g., no insurance compensation), it can be discussed and perhaps eliminated. Generally, psychotherapists are able to conduct their practices with a minimum of record keeping and bookkeeping. As in all aspects of life, the simpler the better. Many psychotherapy patients who are physicians or in business become jealous of how uncomplicated the logistics of a psychotherapy practice are.

CANCELLATIONS

In psychoanalytically oriented psychotherapy, the psychotherapist's primary dedication is to provide continuity. A strong theoretical position can be made for charging for all appointments other than cancellations over which the patient has no control. Detailing the circumstances over which the patient has "no control" (dealings with employers, vacations, automobile problems, business trips, children's care) leads to important interpretable material as the patient and the psychotherapist struggle to understand what constitutes the limits of the patient's control over various aspects of his or her life.

It is striking how many female patients assume that they will interrupt their psychotherapy at the time of their husbands' vacation. Even more startling are the female patients who assume that they will interrupt their own psychotherapy when their husbands' psychoanalysts, particularly those in training psychoanalyses, take their vacation. Discussion of these expectations is remarkably revealing of the multiple, subtle ways a woman may subordinate her self-interest to the needs of her husband. Sometimes revealed are fears, imagined and real, of her husband's anger should she assert her desires. Sometimes her inner disorganization and need to use her husband's life to structure her own become clear.

Contrary to generally held opinion, it is best not to discuss cancellation at the outset, but to let the discussion arise as cancellations occur during the course of the psychotherapy. In the beginning the patient is attending fully to the presenting difficulties and their alleviation. Feelings toward a host of arrangement issues, including cancellation, cannot be anticipated with full force until the situation actively arises in the process of the psychotherapy.

Some psychotherapists articulate cancellation *policies* in advance. Cancellation policies stated in terms of *appropriate* or *sufficient* notice or *acceptable* reasons become judgments and disguised rewards and punishments for ways of behaving. Policies such as "I charge unless I can use the hour" potentially reveal the psychotherapist's situation—such as how busy he is—limiting interpretive work. Psychotherapists who do not charge for canceled appointments often are attempting to avoid, through interaction, the patient's anger and possible retaliation (losing the patient).

Charging for canceled appointments, unless the patient has no control over the cancellation because, say, of illness, minimizes the covert system of reward and punishment, frees patients from an obligation and allows them to choose what to do with a particular hour, keeps information regarding the psychotherapist's situation to a minimum, and allows for lower fees in general. (Theoretically, if one does not charge for missed appointments, the patients who come subsidize the patients who cancel.)

On being told of an impending cancellation, the psychotherapist explores if consideration has been given to the fact that the cancellation interferes with the continuity. When the multiple meanings packed into the situation are worked on in dialogue, an investigation of the reasonableness and fairness of charging for cancellations, if not for that event, then for subsequent cancellations, is initiated. If the patient planned an event before beginning psychotherapy, then the psychotherapist of course does not charge for the cancelled sessions, but work is begun on issues of continuity.

Attention to the reasons for cancelling and its ramifications, particularly with regard to the fee, frequently is misconstrued by the patient as self-serving on the part of the psychotherapist but strikingly decreases the frequency of cancellations. There is a strong compliance aspect as the patient attempts to avoid becoming angry at being charged for missed appointments. As these feelings are made explicit, they become part of the interpretive work, and resolution at various levels is achieved through recognition of the importance of continuity in attaining goals. A distinction frequently has to be drawn between fair and agreeable. One can recognize that something is fair although not to one's liking and consent to something one does not like without feeling demeaned or subjugated.

As the implications of cancellation are discussed and understood, rescheduling compromises can be considered. Patients initially want make-up appointments so as not to feel cheated, and in these interchanges many complex responses are elicited, frequently around the issue of control. It is not a good idea to accumulate a backlog of hours to be "made up." In an intrapsychic sense, a psychotherapy hour cannot "be made up," but an hour can be moved from one week into the next to accommodate an event, maintain the continuity, and minimize the artificiality of make-ups.

Cancellations by the psychotherapist are announced as far in advance as possible. Living a tightly scheduled professional life is a significant hardship that psychotherapists must endure. Coordination of cancellations obviously minimizes interruptions, maximizes continuity, and decreases charges for missed appointments, but it demands that the psychotherapist plan early.

The issue of double charging for a given hour is a complex one clinically and ethically. What does one do if there is a request for a consultation and the hour that is open is one that was cancelled and is being charged for? Psychotherapists generally keep time for consultations, extra appointments, teaching, and administrative matters. If the paid canceled appointment is convenient for a person requesting a consultation, it seems reasonable to use the hour, realizing that, in a sense, one is taking the hour from "another place." Likewise, a "paid-for" hour can be used when a patient asks for an appointment change. The overriding spirit is not to double-charge but to maintain continuity and keep external impingements to a minimum.

ERRORS

Psychotherapists' errors have many meanings and consequences. Errors can be regarded as specific kinds of interactions. They are mistakes or parapraxes, depending on the degree to which they are unconsciously determined.

When the psychotherapist's mistakes about names, dates, appointment times, or relationships are not acknowledged by the patient, the lack of acknowledgment is explored. Subsequently the possible meanings of the psychotherapist's making the error and the possible meanings of the error itself are discussed without confirming the patient's hypotheses.

Parapraxes of all sorts, especially slips of the tongue, by the psychotherapist are revealing. Initially in the psychotherapy, psychotherapists' slips are usually ignored by patients, as are their own. The ignoring, as well as the patient's thoughts about the meaning of the psychotherapist's slip, must be explored. The patient's understanding of the psychotherapist's slip may be closely or only distantly related to the psychotherapist. The plausibility of the patient's conjectures is acknowledged but the patient's understanding of the slip is not confirmed.

Although errors are generally regarded by patients as specific to them, a psychotherapist's errors may be connected with a specific patient, that is, a countertransference or to a class of patients. They may have to do with a mixture of factors related to the patient and the psychotherapist's personal situation, or they may be unrelated to a specific patient or patients but, rather, fully related to the psychotherapist's personal situation. An example of a slip unrelated to a specific patient occurred one spring at the time of an interruption. Meaning to say, "I will see you the day after Memorial Day," I said instead with patient after patient, "I will see you the day after Labor Day."

A complicated situation occurs when two patients come for the same appointment. Generally it is best to take the patient who has come in error into the consultation room while the other waits and discuss briefly the patient's understanding about the confusion. A subsequent appointment is made and at that time the incident is thoroughly analyzed. Psychotherapists should not quickly assume that the error is theirs. The regressive forces operating in the psychotherapeutic situation create a high likelihood that the error is the patient's and is transferentially significant.

If one of the patients is obviously more disturbed, there is theoretical reason to make another appointment for the better integrated patient. Although the situation is troubling to both patients (and often to the psychotherapist), with the better integrated patient the responses can be dealt with in the next appointment. The patient who is not so well integrated is seen so that responses can be dealt with immediately.[3]

When the psychotherapist erroneously has asked a patient to come at the wrong time and there is no clinical reason to see one before the other, the psychotherapist admits the error and apologizes privately to the patient who was wrongly informed. The patient is given a subsequent appointment, when the incident is fully explored. In the session with the patient whose appointment it was, the incident is fully analyzed.

In each situation, if there is no mention of the incident by the patient, the resistance to revealing thoughts is analyzed and the patient's thoughts about the situation, the other patient, and the psychotherapist are detailed. Explanations about the confusion are not offered other than an apology for the inconvenience. Less often than is generally thought an explanation may be necessary with very ill patients. These explanations are essentially a parameter.

It is striking how frequently patients transferentially "cover" psychotherapists' errors, making the error their own to maintain an idealized concept of the psychotherapist, sometimes to cover and defend against hostility. As Ferenczi (1933) wrote, "Instead of contradicting the analyst or accusing him of errors and blindness, the patients *identify themselves with him;* only in rare moments . . . can they . . . protest; normally they do not allow themselves to criticize us, such a criticism does not even become conscious . . ." (p. 158).[4] Yet all too frequently the error becomes a justification for the release of a load of hostility that has accumulated in the psychotherapy and that has deep and intense transference origins.

Psychotherapist errors and slips are extensively explored privately. Psychotherapists' responses to their own errors is of interest. Psychotherapists often feel ashamed of errors revealing an underlying defensive narcissistic investment in not making

---

[3]I have had the experience where both patients were mental health professionals who had heard me lecture on psychoanalytically oriented psychotherapy. More than once, each, sensing the circumstance and excitedly anticipating my response, wished and feared being the "sicker" patient, the one who would remain.

[4]Later in the same paper identification with the aggressor was first described.

errors. Others seem overly eager to "confess" to their patients, wantingit known that they can make errors—a curious narcissistic reversal.

The considerable "movement" in a psychotherapy that follows a psychotherapist's error (especially with confession rather than analysis) has lured more than one psychotherapist into overvaluing the effects of interactive work. The fantasy of purposely making an error and admitting to it as a kind of "corrective" experience is very old in psychotherapy. Always mindful of the narcissistic propensities of psychotherapists, Ferenczi (1933) wrote,

> It would seem to be of advantage occasionally to commit blunders in order to admit afterwards the fault to the patient. This advice is, however, quite superfluous; we commit blunders often enough. One highly intelligent patient became justifiably indignant, saying: 'It would have been much better if you could have avoided blunders altogether. Your vanity, doctor, would like to make profit even out of your errors' [p. 159].

The most difficult errors in psychotherapy are various empathic lapses and errors in concept about psychodynamics and the psychotherapeutic process. Correcting concepts regarding psychodynamics and the psychotherapeutic process is a constant, vital part of psychoanalytically oriented psychotherapy. Yet there are times when the psychotherapist realizes that he or she is lost or grossly mistaken. Although thoughtful reflection is usually corrective, at times it is helpful to "write up" the case. The number of lacunae in facts and understanding that exist even in cases that are fully studied is astonishing. Discussion of cases, often as vignettes illustrating particular situations, in informal consultation groups is of great value in keeping "on track" and in making minor or major corrections in concept. In teaching seminars, it is amazing how frequently inexperienced psychotherapists raise questions about the patients presented by the instructor, the discussion of which is extraordinarily helpful to the instructor. Sometimes formal consultation with another psychotherapist or, less often, referral of the patient to another psychotherapist for consultation or psychotherapy is necessary. *Psychotherapy arises out of dialogue and needs a variety of dialogues to maintain accuracy and clarity.*

It is striking how accurately patients recognize a change in concept, sense a new direction, and directly or indirectly accurately attribute the change to consultation. With surprising frequency the "consultation" appears in the patient's dreams. How much to acknowledge is difficult to decide. Overexplanation is the frequent mistake. Even though the patient's idea of consultation is correct and can be acknowledged, the meanings associated with "consultation" permeate nearly every aspect of the transference and take time to explore, interpret, and integrate.

THE PSYCHOANALYTIC ENVIRONMENT

Too little attention has been paid to the psychoanalytic environment. This lack of attention has many sources and is often justified by the psychoanalytic adage that everything is grist for the mill. Any mill can be overburdened. Key among the environmental necessities are ventilation, sound control, minimum interruptions, confidentiality, and adequate space. The psychotherapist must establish an environment that is quiet, economical, unpretentious, free of interruptions, and consistent. Frequently, unpretentiousness is abused to the point that the surroundings demean the work, the practitioner, and the patient. Langs (1982) has discussed decor in psychotherapy offices. The idea that the "monastic" environment is neutral and ideal has been exploded; there is no neutral environment. It is true that a setting with many items is revealing but not as specifically as alleged. Frequent change of furnishings or of the location of the office is detrimental.

It is nearly impossible for those not involved in psychotherapeutic work, that is, contractors and landlords, to realize how closed a psychotherapy office is. Ventilation is compromised because the door is not opened; there is no movement in the room for 50-minute intervals; and open windows jeopardize sound control. That special care must be given to assure adequate temperature and ventilation is honored largely in the breach.

Sound control and freedom from interruption are of great importance. The work is essentially reflective, requiring minimal distraction. The study of responses to occasional sounds can be useful, but steady disturbing noises make for interactive rather than psychoanalytic work. Voices in which words can be understood are especially detrimental. The sense of confidentiality and safe enclosure is ruptured. The occasional sound of voices is less disturbing and the patient's various responses usable.

The telephone should not be answered during sessions. Answering the telephone during sessions is solely for the convenience of the psychotherapist, usually out of fear of losing referrals. Answering the telephone carries specific and nonspecific risks. It interrupts the session's flow for both patient and psychotherapist. The telephone conversation can be additionally disturbing because of its content. A psychotherapist who is guarded while talking on the telephone risks the caller's wondering what kind of peculiar person is on the other end. The patient identifies with the caller who is trying to talk with this restrained person, while at the same time the patient resents that time is being taken. Although frequently denied, such interaction overwhelms the power of interpretation. Many patients resign themselves to the situation and in despair suppress talking about it, and feelings about the interruption become part of a host of unresolved, unmentioned interactions with varying consequences.

Answering services present many problems because they are geared toward a kind of practice different from a psychotherapy practice and confidentiality is breached. The answering machine has solved many but not all problems for the psychotherapist. The answering machine should be silent (very difficult to find) or in another room. The sound of the mechanism "answering" is an unnecessary disturbance. Patients generally identify with the caller who is not being responded to, and associated feelings enter the limbo of the unmentioned.

The signal system to announce an arriving patient can be designed so that it does not interfere with the current session. Preferably the signal is an announcement light that remains lighted until the psychotherapist turns it off and is in view of the psychotherapist but not of the patient.[5] Time can be inconspicuously monitored if

---

[5]Identifying the subtleties and idiosyncrasies of patients' responses to interruptions is useful. One patient, on hearing the next patient arrive because of a door problem, said, "Well, there is your other patient." The contempt in his words "your other patient" allowed us to analyze his fantasy that I had an unsuccessful practice, just two patients. Further analysis revealed a deeper desire—to be my only patient. The hearing of the "other patient" forced him to admit reluctantly that there was at least one other. As important and appealing as understanding

the clock is placed behind and to one side of the patient's head.

The patient has a right to confidentiality, which requires a separate exit door so that the patient does not have to leave through the waiting room, going past other patients. Similarly, to reduce extra-session influences, the psychotherapist needs access to the office without having to walk through the waiting room. The psychotherapist also should have a private toilet. Long corridors in which patient and psychotherapist walk together from waiting room to treatment room invite difficult interactions.

The chairs should be conveniently arranged and a small table placed by the patient's chair with tissues. A young male psychotherapist in supervision tells of an amusing incident regarding tissue. The episode illustrates the importance of attention to the psychotherapeutic environment. The patient was an older, maternal woman who immediately began to cry and said, "Oh dear, I don't have a handkerchief, do you have one?" The psychotherapist did not have tissues for the patient and, unsure what to do, reached into his pocket and brought forth his handkerchief. The hour continued with the patient using his handkerchief. At the end of the hour the patient said, "Oh I must take this home and launder it for you." At the next hour, the psychotherapist was presented with the handkerchief in a box with a ribbon. He took it, and the patient began talking. Soon she was crying. "Oh, may I use the handkerchief again?" she asked. The box was handed to her. Thus was set up an unfortunate series of interactions that could have been obviated by thoughtfulness in providing the essentials of the environment.

The presence of the psychoanalytic couch in the office of a psychotherapist who is also a psychoanalyst generally goes unmentioned in psychotherapy until, in response to the patient's preconscious representations, the psychotherapist calls it to the patient's attention. This confrontation may begin the exploration of the various meanings of psychotherapy and psychoanalysis to the patient. These explorations are critical in their mutual consideration of converting psychoanalytically oriented psychotherapy into psychoanalysis (Fisher, 1987; Gill, 1988).

The absence of the couch from the office of the psychotherapist who is not a psychoanalyst becomes another of the innumerable

---

gleaned from such responses is, it loses its power and immediacy if interruptions occur often.

interactions that unfortunately seldom find their way into the material even in psychoanalytically oriented psychotherapy. All too often the situation is one in which a psychotherapist, reluctant to discuss the differences between psychotherapy and psychoanalysis—in fact not wishing to discuss his lack of psychoanalytic training—is colluding with the patient, who is grateful not to have to consider psychoanalysis.

Important considerations regarding what to call the patient are related to control issues, various kinds of competition, and levels of familiarity on both sides. In general, it is best to learn to deal with patients without calling them anything. To assume that patients want their psychotherapists and themselves to be on a first-name basis often reflects the psychotherapist's conflicts after professionalism or is arrogance masquerading as egalitarianism.

When I first meet a patient in the waiting room, I introduce myself as Dr. Oremland and extend my hand. Thus I establish that I am to be called Dr. Oremland, a specific interaction, and avoid calling the patient anything specifically. When patients are called on the telephone, an infrequent occurrence in a well-run psychotherapy practice, they are called by their last names with their proper title, Dr., Mr., Mrs., Ms. Often a discussion ensues in the next hour about "Why don't you call me Bill?" Discussing how the psychotherapist and patient are to address each other often adds insight into the difference between dealing with people as equals and dealing with everyone identically. These discussions are highly relevant to issues of esteem, control, subjugation, and competition. As with most aspects of psychoanalytically oriented psychotherapy, it is better to wait until situations arise and analyze them in the context of the transference.

Patients are not extensively greeted on each visit, nor is a handshake offered at the beginning or end of sessions. Male psychotherapists do not help female patients with their coats or with the door. All this is done in an atmosphere of respect, and neutral friendliness without stiffness or aloofness.

When a significant interruption is initiated by the patient or me, I offer my hand at the end of the last session and say, "I hope it goes well." When patients return, I shake hands and say, "It is good to see you again." Because I am careful not to label interruptions as other than interruptions, I have had more than one good-spirited patient say to me, "Have a good interruption."

GIFTS, LETTERS, AND
ACCIDENTAL MEETINGS

Patients may bring gifts for their psychotherapists. Giving gifts is an acting out of feelings of idealization, obligation, gratitude, dependency, and at times hostility. Kohut (1971) helped distinguish various kinds of idealizations, which previously had been seen largely as expressions of hostility.

The gift is examined, commented upon, and returned to analyze why it is being given. Patients universally feel rejected; yet, as they recognize the underlying meaning of the giving, they realize the importance of understanding. Gifts at termination are of a different order. They are appreciated and often cherished.

On occasion patients may present an important document for the psychotherapist to read. Such a presentation may be an attempt to make the psychotherapist responsible for decisions or to idealize the psychotherapist into a pan-expert. The psychotherapist peruses what is presented and inquires why it is shown rather than talked about. Letters to the patient often are presented to conceal that the patient is afraid that the psychotherapist does not fully appreciate how difficult a situation is. The emphasis in the session is on understanding why the patient thinks that the psychotherapist does not understand. At times, the patient hopes that the psychotherapist will see that the patient is wrong and that the situation is not as bad as portrayed.

Chance extrasession meetings between the patient and the psychotherapist occur. If the meeting involves the psychotherapist's family, introducing family members may, on occasion, be called for. Such meetings are neutral, warm, brief, and fully discussed in the next session. If the patient does not mention it, which is rare, the psychotherapist does. Sometimes a meeting is anticipated and can be discussed. Often while the significance of such a meeting is being analyzed, the patient may feel unready to talk about it and avoids the possibility. Interestingly, some psychotherapists are uncomfortable meeting patients outside the session, and some even eschew attending certain events for that reason. Such discomfort represents countertransference overvaluations in need of careful scrutiny.

Psychoanalytically Oriented Psychotherapy and Psychoanalysis: A Double Helix

Letter to Max Delbrück:

March 12, 1953

Dear Max:
The basic features of the model are (1) the basic structure is helical—it consists of two intertwining helices . . . (2) the helices are not identical but complementary. . . . The screw is right handed. . . .

Jim

(*The Double Helix,* James D. Watson, 1968)

Thus far I have developed a line of thought that distinguishes the psychoanalytic orientation common to psychoanalytically oriented psychotherapy and psychoanalysis from the orientation of interactive psychotherapy. This polarity is a refinement of the polarity between psychoanalysis and psychotherapy described in 1982 by Merton Gill. My discussion stems from seeing Gill's psychoanalysis as too inclusive: within his psychoanalysis a psychoanalytically oriented psychotherapy can be differentiated from psychoanalysis proper.

Distinguishing psychoanalytically oriented psychotherapy from psychoanalysis establishes a new triad of psychotherapies guided by psychoanalytic theory: *interactive psychotherapy, psychoanalytically oriented psychotherapy, and psychoanalysis.* This triad is reminiscent of, but different from, Gill's 1954 triad of *psychotherapy, intermediate form, and psychoanalysis* and the current, commonly used triad of *supportive psychotherapy, exploratory psychotherapy, and psychoanalysis.*

The essential commonality between psychoanalytically oriented psychotherapy and psychoanalysis resides in the intervention employed, that is, interpretation. The essential difference lies in the primary area of psychotherapeutic interplay. In broad sweep, the *operational* difference between psychoanalytically oriented psychotherapy and psychoanalysis is the training of the practitioner, the range of patients treated, the frequency of sessions, and the use of the couch. Simply put, the mode (interpretation) is the same; the modalities and what eventuates as the process unfolds is different.

The terms *modality* and *mode,* borrowed from Erik Erikson (1959), are extended and used here in specific ways. Modality refers to a psychotherapy procedure with specific dimensions. Mode refers to the predominant intervention of the procedure. Hence, even though the modes of psychoanalysis and of psychoanalytically oriented psychotherapy are identical, (interpretation), the modalities are different owing to other factors, such as frequency of visits, positioning, and patient selection.

Although interactive psychotherapy and psychoanalytically oriented psychotherapy have similarities (face–to–face positioning, broad patient population, broad practitioner training), the mode differs (interactive versus interpretive). Briefly put, the mode is the same in psychoanalysis and in psychoanalytically oriented psychotherapy; the modalities are different. With interactive psychotherapy and psychoanalytically oriented psychotherapy, the modes and the modalities are different.

RANGE OF PATIENTS

Psychoanalytically oriented psychotherapy arose out of the attempt to treat very disturbed patients psychoanalytically (Fromm-Reichmann, 1950). As clinical experience with psychoanalytically oriented psychotherapy increased and as psychoanalytic theory developmentally and psychodynamically differentiated the nosological spectrum of psychopathology, the range of patients treated with psychoanalytically oriented psychotherapy and with psychoanalysis increased (Stone, 1954; Kernberg, 1967, 1968).

As previously discussed, nosological specificity for the psychotherapy modalities is only roughly applicable, yet experience supports the general view that few psychotics can be treated with psychoanalysis and more with psychoanalytically oriented psychotherapy; that only some patients with borderline disorders can be treated with psychoanalysis, and many more can be treated with psychoanalytically oriented psychotherapy; and that many neurotics and patients with character disorders can be treated with psychoanalysis and even more with psychoanalytically oriented psychotherapy. Yet, because the patient population that is treatable with psychoanalytically oriented psychotherapy is far broader than the population that can be treated with psychoanalysis proper, and the range of practitioners practicing psychoanalytic psychotherapy is far broader than that practicing psychoanalysis, empirically valid comparisons of course and outcome among interactive, psychotherapy, psychoanalytically oriented psychotherapy, and psychoanalysis present difficulties (Wallerstein, 1986).

My discussion omits large groups of patients of vast clinical and sociological importance, including acting out characters, substance abusers, and the variety of severely characteriologically and sociologically disturbed people who can at times be treated with psychoanalytically oriented psychotherapy within extensive parameters, edicts and injunctions regarding specific behaviors in and outside the sessions, but seldom with psychoanalysis (Eissler, 1953). Generally the similarities and differences between psychoanalytically oriented psychotherapy and psychoanalysis are brought to light better if the discussion is limited to patients for whom either modality is applicable.

TRAINING AND PSYCHOANALYTICALLY ORIENTED PSYCHOTHERAPY

Training in psychotherapy is largely clinical apprenticeship. It suffers from a lack of systematization, particularly in theory. Because of vast recent shifts in training in psychiatry, psychology, and social work, as other interests have impinged on the curriculum, the singular place of psychoanalytic theory and psychotherapy in the training of the mental health professions has been eroded. Training in psychotherapy for all three fields is rapidly becoming a postgraduate activity. Equally applicable to training in psychoanalytically oriented psychotherapy and to training in psychoanalysis is the tripartite model of seminars in theory and continuous case conferences, supervision, and personal psychotherapy. Ideally training for psychoanalytically oriented psychotherapy and for psychoanalysis should be identical in theory of development, personality, psychopathology, metapsychology, and technique.

Training in the technique of psychoanalytically oriented psychotherapy involves extensive supervision of individual cases and, concurrent with individual supervision, continuous case conferences for group discussion of the unfolding psychoanalytically oriented psychotherapy process. Because of the greater heterogeneity of the cases suitable for psychoanalytically oriented psychotherapy than for psychoanalysis, specific supervised work with borderline and psychotic patients is important.

The question of personal psychotherapy is complex. Because of the vagaries of training and a long tradition (as well as certain proprietary interests), personal psychotherapy is closely aligned with training for psychoanalytic psychotherapies. Many reasons support the view that personal psychotherapy should be outside the purview of a training program and that the sole measure of progression in training should be performance in seminars and supervision; this viewpoint raises the question of whether or not personal psychotherapy should be required. Although the case for personal psychotherapy has strong support, many excellent, attuned, skillful psychotherapists have not had personal psychotherapy.[1]

---

[1]The experience at the San Francisco Institute for Psychoanalytic Psychotherapy and Psychoanalysis, where personal psychotherapy is not required for those in training in psychotherapy (although it is for those in training in psychoanalysis), is that nearly all the trainees are in or early seek personal psychotherapy. Our experience is that whether or not a student in training in psychotherapy seeks psychoanalysis or psychotherapy is related to, among other factors, prior educational experience, primarily how prominent psychoanalysis and psychoanalysts were in the trainees' training institutions.

In training for psychoanalytically oriented psychotherapy, it is difficult to decide if the personal psychotherapy required or recommended should be psychoanalytically oriented psychotherapy or psychoanalysis. That this issue cannot be categorically answered is closely related to indications for psychoanalytically oriented psychotherapy and psychoanalysis, discussed later.

FREQUENCY OF SESSIONS

Frequency of sessions in any psychotherapy ideally is determined by the psychotherapist. Psychotherapy, because of its greater range of applicability, is always subject to socioeconomic constraints. Unfortunately psychotherapy too often "happens" because of the psychotherapist's limitations (not having been trained as a psychoanalyst), time restrictions, and the patient's financial circumstances. In short, psychotherapy is often a repository when clear distinctions have not been made.

In general, in psychotherapy, the qualitative differences in the work between once-a-week and twice-weekly sessions are greater than those between any other incremental increase. The increase to twice-a-week treatment shifts the patient's engagement from a weekly request to bear witness to, or to correct, the events of his or her life to a beginning effort at introspection. Once-a-week psychotherapy frequently becomes interactive regardless of the psychotherapist's orientation or the nature of the psychotherapist's interventions.

Experience supports the practice of psychoanalysis four or five times a week (seldom three times a week) and psychoanalytically oriented psychotherapy twice a week. Psychoanalytically oriented psychotherapy can be as frequent as seven times or more a week when the patient's object constancy is so impaired that transferential *continuities* cannot be maintained.

Unfortunately for psychotherapists, severely disturbed patients who are able to maintain a fragile sense of the psychotherapist during the week often cannot on weekends. During the week, strengthened by the experience of seeing the psychotherapist in the office in the professional role, the patient can better maintain be-

tween sessions the concrete idea (a fragile intrapsychic representation) that the psychotherapist is in the office and seemingly available. The weekend engenders a nearly unlimited range of
imaginings regarding the psychotherapist, and the disturbed patient may lose all sense of the psychotherapist's "being there"
(intrapsychically represented) and become disorganized.

As patients reconstitute, the threat of the weekend changes. With
improvement, more specific fantasies form, such as the psychotherapist's being with family. These fantasies are often laced with
intense anger and jealousy. Although disturbing in a different way
to the patient (and at times to the psychotherapist), such emotion-
laden, specific fantasies about the psychotherapist are beginning
manifestations of emerging and reconstituted object constancy. At
this point, as the significance of the fantasies is interpreted and new
understanding integrated, the frequency of the appointments can be
reduced. Psychoanalytically oriented psychotherapy at this level of
frequency, as with patients who require extensive use of parameters, is a special situation of great clinical importance but is not
a good example for general discussion.

It is worth reiterating that there is a fundamental difference
between seeing a patient frequently to provide a sense of continuity
and a feeling that the psychotherapist "is there"—an interaction—
and seeing a patient frequently because the patient's capacity to
maintain a sense of object constancy is so fragile that an interpretive
line cannot be established to *understand* the distortions in feelings
that interfere with a continuing sense that the psychotherapist "is
there." This distinction highlights essential differences between the
interactive approach—an attempt to provide a feeling—and the
psychoanalytic orientation—an attempt to understand a feeling.

Although never put to empirical verification, in psychoanaliti-
cally oriented psychotherapy and psychoanalysis, *increased frequency
generally increases the detailing of the study of the interplay without changing
the area of interplay*. This raises a difficult question: why not see
patients in psychoanalytically oriented psychotherapy more frequently than twice a week to increase the fineness of the work? At
the moment, our answer comes from experience, tradition, and the
overriding rule of psychotherapy: be as economical with respect
to the patient's time and financial resources as possible. The discussion of increasing frequency in psychoanalytically oriented

psychotherapy takes us into the murky area of indications for psychoanalytically oriented psychotherapy versus indications for psychoanalysis, a subject considered later.

THE COUCH

Lore has it that Freud, continuing the tradition of hypnosis, began seeing patients on the couch because of a distaste for being looked at hour after hour. Whatever Freud's reasons, experience has shown that the simple device of having the patient lie on the couch, with the psychotherapist outside of view, has a marked effect on what is brought forth in the patient's thoughts, particularly when the meetings are nearly daily. Without the interacting, correcting, at times remarkably subtle, reactions that are part and parcel of face-to-face communication, the patient's verbalization falls somewhere between soliloquy and dialogue. Thoughts are more reflective and meditative, with switches in topics and swings between fantasies and actualities. With use of the couch and sufficient frequency of sessions, thoughts about the psychoanalyst tend to be more fleeting and fantasy laced than in face-to-face work. Concrete thinking and affective storms increase, and transference enactments intensify. The composite picture is complex and is usually termed regressive; when more specific, it is called the transference neurosis (Arlow, 1975).

Given the propensity of some psychotherapists to use the couch regardless of their understanding of the process, the role of the couch in psychoanalytically oriented psychotherapy requires special discussion. Unfortunately, often the unstated reason for using the couch in psychotherapies is the status afforded the practitioner and the patient by the patient's being "on the couch." Stated reasons include relaxing the patient, making the patient less aware of the psychotherapist's responses, and encouraging free association.

Using the couch for these reasons is interactive and not psychoanalytic. Bolstering the patient's (and the psychotherapist's) self-esteem or attempting to fulfill patient expectations by using the couch is to use interaction for therapeutic purposes. Relaxing the patient raises the question, relaxing the patient for what? In psycho-

analytically oriented psychotherapy, the major area of psychotherapeutic interest is the detailed study of the complexity of the
patient's way of relating to the psychotherapist rather than inducing
a situation in which the patient can talk more easily. Likewise,
attempts to induce free association reflect confused ideas about the
nature and place of free association in any therapeutic modality,
including psychoanalysis.

The reader can easily anticipate how strongly I oppose the practice of placing patients in psychoanalytically oriented psychotherapy on the couch. The justifications essentially stem from
confusion about transference, resistance, and the nature of the
psychoanalytic orientation and from countertransference. Inas-
much as psychoanalytically oriented psychotherapy, as will be
considered, is a detailed investigation of the interpersonal interaction between patient and psychotherapist, the use of the couch in
psychoanalytically oriented psychotherapy deprives the patient of
the immediacy of face-to-face contact and the specific opportunity
that psychoanalytically oriented psychotherapy affords to maxi-
mize the discovery of transferences in the actualities of the interaction. The psychotherapist who uses the couch for psychoanalytically oriented psychotherapy intensifies the limitations of that
modality and of psychoanalysis and offers the patient the weaker
aspect of each.

AREA OF INTERPLAY

The most important consideration differentiating psychoanalytically oriented psychotherapy from psychoanalysis is the area of the
psychotherapeutic interplay, which in Bernard Bandler's terms,
"involves a different terrain from . . . psychoanalysis" (cited in
English, 1965, p. 550). Although there is *marked overlap* between
them, the two modalities move the patient's interests in different
directions, dictated by the lack of direct visual contact with the
psychoanalyst (the couch) and enhanced by increased frequency. In
psychoanalytically oriented psychotherapy the actualities of the
interaction dominate, and there is exquisite dissection of the trans-

ference in the interaction. In psychoanalysis, the actualities of the interaction are less immediate, and conjecture increases and reifies.

In other words, in both psychoanalytically oriented psychotherapy and psychoanalysis there is within the external dialogue a specific kind of internal soliloquy. The soliloquy is itself a complex intrapsychic "conversation" among longitudinal and cross-sectional aspects of the self, with various externalizations and displacements interacting with, and being organized by, the external dialogue.

In psychoanalytically oriented psychotherapy, the internal soliloquy remains more integrally a part of the external dialogue than in psychoanalysis. The interpretations in psychoanalytically oriented psychotherapy progressively reveal the internal soliloquy within the external dialogue, more specifically the transference within the actualities of the interplay. In psychoanalysis, as the internal soliloquy intensifies through interpretation of the resistances, the historical aspects of the life experience predominate. Essentially each modality explores different areas of the interplay. Yet in both a past is located that enriches the present. In both, the future is determined by a fuller understanding of the present. In both the here-and-now becomes multidimensional.[2]

Detailing of the difference between psychoanalytically oriented psychotherapy and psychoanalysis is further complicated by the fact that the past that is remembered and reconstructed in any psychotherapist–patient or psychoanalyst–patient dyad at a particular time is *a past,* but one of many pasts. Psychoanalysts and psychotherapists alike tend to regard the past that emerges in their patient dyad as the only past. Even so, the past as reconstructed in a

---

[2]The here-and-now is a concept of considerable interest. The idea arose largely in social work in the 1960s as an attempt to recapture the casework orientation and free clinical social work from the then prevalent tendency to ape the techniques of psychoanalysis. In the social case work here-and-now, the case worker directs the interview toward evaluation of what is happening to the client (patient) at that moment in the client's life outside the sessions and what the client is doing about it. The social worker is actively involved in a here-and-now, but one markedly different from the immediacy of the transferential interpersonal interaction. Social workers' exploration of their here-and-now permits a highly skilled and effective counseling technique that may or may not be psychoanalytically guided.

psychoanalysis is generally a more detailed, verifiable one than that which emerges in psychoanalytically oriented psychotherapy.

Simply put, it is a different experience with different eventualities to talk face-to-face with someone than to talk with someone when response dynamics are markedly limited. Yet the goals sought by way of the different paths are similar if not identical: as full an understanding of the personality as possible within the modality.

Many psychoanalysts, without so articulating, consider psycho-analysis to be the fullest possible psychotherapy—that psychoanal-ysis does more in every sphere—and will reject this differentiation between the modalities. They can only see the modalities compar-atively, that is, as superior and inferior, complete or incomplete, rather than complementary, as modalities with different quantita-tive emphases.

Yet any given patient in psychoanalysis may keep the material closely aligned to the actualities in the interaction; and any given patient in psychoanalytically oriented psychotherapy may exten-sively detail the past. The peril to psychoanalytically oriented psy-chotherapy is that it can become poor psychoanalysis. The peril to psychoanalysis is that it can become poor psychoanalytically ori-ented psychotherapy. A peril common to both is that the psycho-analytic orientation is lost and they will become disguised interac-tive psychotherapy.

THE QUESTION OF INCOMPLETENESS

Traditionally psychoanalysts and psychotherapists consider psy-chotherapy as an incomplete mode when compared with psychoanalysis.[3] The most critical opponents see psychotherapy as merely ventilative and supportive; those who endorse it see it as symptom alleviating with limited goals. The years have seen an increasing albeit reluctant recognition that psychotherapy brings about significant and lasting personality change.

---

[3] In this discussion of incompleteness, I use the term psychotherapy loosely; and, as usually defined, the variety of suggestive, exploring, face-to-face, psychoana-lytically guided psychotherapies that are regarded as distinct from psychoanalysis.

The question of incompleteness in psychotherapy opens a Pandora's box. When a patient is equally suitable for either modality, usually the choice is made because of the patient's financial limitations or the psychotherapist's lack of training in psychoanalysis. Although lip service is paid to the idea that patients suitable for psychoanalysis should be referred for psychoanalysis, in fact, few patients are referred by psychotherapists for psychoanalysis, even though psychotherapists often seek psychoanalysis for themselves. (More recently the situation has been changing as many psychotherapists seek psychotherapy rather than psychoanalysis for themselves. Some, with chauvinistic pride, actively eschew psychoanalysis.)

If psychotherapy is the lesser modality, or incomplete, important ethical considerations are raised. Can any profession, particularly one of the healing arts, maintain high ethical standards if it condones offering lesser or incomplete treatment because of the patient's financial or the practitioner's technical limitations? Such ethical considerations pose a more pressing problem to psychoanalysts than psychotherapists because psychoanalysts generally are dedicated to the proposition that psychoanalysis is the preferred treatment for the suitable patient. Yet when psychoanalysis is recommended, it frequently means less per-hour remuneration. In a sense all patients in psychoanalysis are seen at a reduced hourly fee. A patient who agrees to come four times a week at a certain fee may accept a higher fee for less frequent sessions, particularly if he or she is uninformed. Freud (1913) early in his work recognized the discrepancy in remuneration for those practicing psychoanalysis and for other specialists: "In fixing his fee the analyst must also allow for the fact that, hard as he may work, he can never earn as much as other [psychotherapists]" (p. 132).

The psychoanalyst frequently faces difficult choices: seeing the patient in psychoanalysis at a reduced hourly fee; referring the patient to another psychoanalyst, usually a younger colleague, who traditionally has a lower hourly fee, or seeing the patient less frequently in psychotherapy at a higher hourly fee.

Experience has shown that referring a patient to younger colleagues of the three mental health professions so that the patient can be seen at a greater frequency in psychoanalytically oriented psychotherapy or in psychoanalysis results in the patient's being seen less frequently at higher fees. Although the fee issue is less critical in clinics of psychoanalytic institutes, referral to psychoanalytic clinics remains more a theoretical than a practical solution because of the host of additional problems incurred in such referrals.

The issue of referral is less acute for psychotherapists. Because psychotherapists often have unclear concepts regarding psychoanalysis, they seldom view psychoanalysis as being indicated, and there is not the ethical question of psychotherapy versus psychoanalysis. There is, however, the parallel, albeit seldom discussed, consideration of seeing patients once a week at a higher fee when they should be seen twice a week.

The ethical issues regarding providing a lesser treatment are more obvious in these days of "full disclosure" than they were a decade ago, when for complex sociohistorical reasons there was essentially a conspiracy of silence among mental health professionals regarding these issues. Yet these ethical concerns must not be considered only in a self-serving context. They must also be considered in the context of the imprecision that colors indications and goals for all the psychotherapies including psychoanalysis.

The question of incompleteness of psychotherapy versus psychoanalysis has not been clarified by various attempts at empirical study (see Wallerstein, 1968, 1986; Horowitz et al., 1984; Luborsky, 1988). Such studies are plagued by unclear and multiple definitions of goals, improvement, sustained change, and difficulties in providing comparable cases and comparable practitioners. Generally, existing studies and most clinical experience do not give psychoanalysis, even for equally suitable cases, a clear-cut therapeutic supremacy over the psychotherapies. Most investigations, echoing the experiences of clinicians, attest to broader sustained personality change from psychotherapy than traditionally espoused (Wallerstein, 1986).

A clinical experience illustrates the situation. A man in his 40s, who had a Ph.D. in engineering and a M.B.A. from a prestigious university and was the head of a major venture capital firm that specialized in researching high-technology companies, consulted me for severe, long-standing depression, feelings of inadequacy, and difficulty in relating to his wife and children. After some evaluating sessions, I suggested that he consider psychoanalysis. (As the reader will discover, I have since changed this way of proceeding.) Although he knew little about psychotherapy or psychoanalysis, he asked a number of relevant and difficult-to-answer questions.

At the next session, he produced a bound report that the research department of his company had prepared at his request. As he handed me the report, he said with a wry smile, "I can tell you that there isn't a study that indicates with any validity a significant outcome difference between the two. In fact, there is not a study that indicates with any validity that either makes any kind of difference. I can also tell you that the way you guys are going about it, you are never going to find out." He decided on psychoanalysis because it made sense to him that more frequent sessions increased the likelihood of a better result. Fortunately, he had a good result.

The various psychotherapies should not be evaluated solely on the basis of therapeutic efficacy. As discussed in Chapter 2, goals other than improvement, however sustained, must be considered. It seems likely that as long as behavioral improvement in the therapeutic sense is the primary goal (a triumph for the therapeutic), the therapeutically oriented psychotherapies, those *designed* to produce specific changes, will present themselves as equal to, if not superior to, those which maintain the psychoanalytic orientation. From the limited therapeutic perspective, it seems likely that of all the psychotherapies, interactive psychotherapy, whether psychoanalytically guided or not, is the most widely effective. This question raises moral as well as therapeutic issues.

> The insight therapist, by the same token, may propose to start on the motivational path suggested by the symptoms which confront him without prejudice as to where it will lead, with only the faith that it will lead somewhere worth going. But in so doing, he effectively abandons the elementary notions of treatment and cure . . . for all practical purposes, he makes of insight an end unto itself, which, . . . forces a redefinition of his work; . . . one that casts him in the mold of a secular moralist. . . . [the psychotherapist] is trying to sell something other than what the patient intended to buy is morally questionable. . . . In any case, the point here is not so much one of establishing professional ethics, as of assessing the very nature of the profession [London, 1964, pp. 62, 63].

With regard to psychoanalytically oriented psychotherapy and psychoanalysis, we must eventually evaluate, as difficult as it will be, the enduring significance of the qualitatively different "aftereducations" of the two modalities.

INDICATIONS FOR PSYCHOANALYTICALLY
ORIENTED PSYCHOTHERAPY

Clinical experience supports the contention that psychoanalytically oriented psychotherapy is more suitable than psychoanalysis for large numbers of psychotics, most borderlines, and nearly all neurotics and patients with character disorders who are considered unanalyzable.[4] Psychoanalytically oriented psychotherapy may also be indicated over psychoanalysis for people seeking second psychoanalyses and certainly for those seeking third psychoanalyses.

"Unanalyzable neurotic" is a catch-all phrase that describes patients who are apparently neurotic but who do poorly in their psychoanalyses. The failure is usually attributed to the patients' poor motivation, high resistance, or not being psychologically minded. Many such "failed cases" are people who were incorrectly diagnosed as neurotic when in actuality they were borderline personalities with rigid obsessive-compulsive symptoms who should have been in psychoanalytically oriented psychotherapy and not in psychoanalysis.

Yet some "unanalyzable neurotics" are people who were involved in psychoanalyses in which initial working on transference resistance was inadequate, or they were unwitting victims of countertransference problems. When they are seen in psychoanalytically oriented psychotherapy, it may become apparent that some of these people could again be in psychoanalysis. For a variety of reasons this proposal may or may not be presented to the patient. Even

---

[4]The differentiation of psychotics and borderlines who can be psychoanalyzed takes us into a difficult area that is more properly a part of technical discussions of psychoanalysis. Experience suggests that the psychoanalysis of psychotics and borderlines is so individual that it must be decided case by case, probably more accurately, therapeutic dyad by therapeutic dyad. It is likely that in most successful cases, the process in effect is a four- or five-times-a-week psychoanalytically oriented psychotherapy on the couch or is a disguised interactive psychotherapy.

when it is presented, many continue their psychoanalytically oriented psychotherapies and complete the work with apparently satisfactory results, supporting the view that there is considerable therapeutic overlap of the modalities.

PATIENTS WHO ARE EQUALLY SUITABLE FOR PSYCHOANALYSIS AND FOR PSYCHOANALYTICALLY ORIENTED PSYCHOTHERAPY

Thus far the discussion of indications for psychoanalytically oriented psychotherapy as opposed to psychoanalysis has not directly addressed the issue of the patient who is equally suitable for either modality. If it is true that psychoanalytically oriented psychotherapy offers a more complete understanding of interpersonal interaction through its detailed study of the complexity of the actualities of relationship and that psychoanalysis offers a more complete reconstruction of the important developmental events determining character and symptom formation, then *each modality in a sense is incomplete.* Yet there seems to be sufficient clinical overlap so that each modality is "therapeutically" equally efficacious. Considered in terms of the psychoanalytic orientation, Freud's after-education, each modality develops a great deal of vital, pertinent, and potentially mutative material but with different, although overlapping, emphases. In short, each offers a different, although overlapping, "after-education."

From these perspectives, neither psychoanalytically oriented psychotherapy nor psychoanalysis viewed narrowly, for therapeutic efficacy, or broadly, as an aftereducation, offers less than the other. This view of efficacy, although it does not help to establish which modality to offer to the patient who is equally suitable for either, does provide a theoretical rationale for a way of proceeding that remains true to the psychoanalytic orientation.

I begin with all patients in ad hoc psychoanalytically oriented psychotherapy sessions. Although it may seem contradictory, as previously discussed, I prefer psychoanalysis over psychoanalytically oriented psychotherapy for the patient who is equally suitable for either, because I see the historical/genetic orientation as more generic and potentially better able to be generalized than the cross-sectional, dynamic orientation.[5]

Even though some patients come with such an informed predisposition toward psychoanalysis that the period of psychoanalytically oriented psychotherapy is quite short, with the usual patient I begin the consideration of regularity and frequency of sessions during the initial, ad hoc evaluation.[6] As concerns about increased frequency and regularity are interpreted within the transference and clarifications are initiated, I suggest regular, twice-a-week, face-to-face sessions.

As the face-to-face psychoanalytically oriented process develops, conscious and preconscious manifestations of the fear, need, and desire for "more" frequently present themselves. Conscious expression of desires for increased frequency, use of the couch, and for psychoanalysis is a mixture of actual considerations and specific transference enactments regarding intimacy, commitment, competition, sexuality, and a host of related vicissitudes of interpersonal relatedness that must be investigated. There is much to "unpack" in the request to be in psychoanalysis.

More cryptic manifestations of desires for increased frequency are statements such as "I don't know where to begin. There is so much," or "It is hardly worth beginning; it is overwhelming." Silence itself may be a manifestation of desire for more. An interpretation such as "You're quiet because you want much and are

---

[5]I fully acknowledge this as a biased opinion based on a general view of what influences thinking (education) and on personal experience including the ethos in which I was trained.

[6]The term "usual patient" needs explanation. Not surprisingly, as the prestige of psychoanalysis has decreased, fewer people overtly desire or have accurate ideas about psychoanalysis. Frequently the term psychoanalysis is used interchangeably with the terms psychotherapy and therapy, and all are used imprecisely and interchangeably with analysis. Those aspects of psychoanalysis which are obviously differentiating—four-times-a-week frequency, use of the couch, and lessened interactive interventions—are seen as outmoded procedures that have been replaced by "newer techniques." Increasingly, successive generations of mental health professionals have ideas regarding psychoanalysis that are similar to the "usual patient." It is a frequent error to assume that mental health professionals know more than they do about psychotherapy, psychoanalysis, or themselves than the "usual patient."

afraid you'll be disappointed," shows a relation between the silence and a conflicted desire for "more."

It is important to keep in mind that when desires for increased frequency are interpreted in psychoanalytically oriented psychotherapy, the interpretation furthers the process and does not invariably mean that an increase in frequency and a shift to psychoanalysis are warranted. Just as the frequently voiced "I really don't want anything long or involved" or desires to interrupt do not necessarily mean that the patient will not continue, the fear of, and desire for, increased frequency has meanings beyond a request for more hours or a shift in modality. These thoughts parallel the overt and covert requests by patients in psychoanalysis to be in psychotherapy. *Generally, interpretation of such requests intensifies the modality rather than resulting in a change of modality.*

It is difficult to specify the determinants in those situations in which interpretation of a variety of conflicts associated with a desire for increased intensity results in the patient's changing from psychoanalytically oriented psychotherapy to psychoanalysis. Factors beyond resistance play a role, including identification with the practitioner, other identifications, early educational experiences with psychoanalysis, and a host of reasons that are idiosyncratic to the psychotherapeutic dyad.

At this point in the process, as resistance manifestations—conflicts over intimacy, commitment, competitiveness, and sexuality—are identified and interpreted in the context of the transference, the issue of frequency is reevaluated and the practical considerations are reviewed.[7] For the patient who is equally suitable for either modal-

---

[7]For the patient for whom psychoanalysis is contraindicated but for whom frequency must be increased to maintain object constancy, there may be pressure for psychoanalysis (usually use of the couch). At that time, the pressure for psychoanalysis must be interpreted in terms of transference. If the patient persists and insists on psychoanalysis, the psychotherapist's reluctance must be explained (a parameter) and the transferential aspect of the response interpreted. Such patients are often mental health professionals who at some level recognize that they are borderline or psychotic. The wish to be in psychoanalysis may be an attempt to deny what they fear. If the psychotherapist enters into this collusion, the treatment frequently becomes a supportive interaction. Although it is often said that manifest psychosis may be precipitated by psychoanalysis, in practice this is extraordinarily rare. The all-too-frequent result of this kind of alliance is that the treatment is unending. Most often such unfortunate situations arise from faulty diagnosis,

ity, I equally favor continuing the psychoanalytically oriented psychotherapy or increasing frequency and beginning psychoanalysis. If there is agreement to increasing sessions to four times a week, I suggest that we begin on the couch while the schedule is worked out.

Usually there is considerable, specific, interpretable material presented largely in the transference context regarding the couch, perhaps even more than that associated with increasing frequency. Often the desire to use the couch is uncovered as a resistance; for example, embarrassing material can be presented without the patients having to look at the psychotherapist, and feelings of shame can thus be avoided.

It is fascinating to observe the difference in the material that emerges when the use of the couch is discussed in psychoanalytically oriented psychotherapy and, if use of the couch ensues, subsequently in psychoanalysis. Although there is considerable overlap, generally the material in the former retains the interpersonal features characteristic of that modality, whereas in psychoanalysis the material takes on a stronger personal narrative quality. This discussion is not to suggest that one sphere is preferable to the other, but rather that, although the mode is the same, the modalities are different.

This incremental, interpretive way of proceeding allows for the identification, discussion, and interpretation of the *meaning* of the technical characteristics of ideas associated with the modalities themselves at each step in the process. Regardless of which modality eventuates, anything short of full discussion, interpretation, and beginning integration of the meaning surrounding the proposed changes—including the patient's quick offer of or agreement to four-times-a-week sessions, use of the couch, scheduling arrangements, fee, cancellation policies, and instructions to free associate—is seen as an acting out in which the psychoanalyst is colluding. This way of proceeding operationally resembles Gill's (1988) discussion of intensification in psychoanalysis.

When the psychotherapist proceeds incrementally, patients outside the mental health field tend to continue in psychoanalytically

---

overeagerness on the part of the practitioner to have patients in psychoanalysis, and transference–countertransference collusions.

oriented psychotherapy, seeing it as the more conservative choice. Mental health professionals, on the other hand, tend to select psychoanalysis because of the greater prestige that psychoanalysis carries within the field itself. These tendencies, which largely are disguised transference–countertransference imperatives, transcend the thoroughness of the interpretive investigation of the various factors involved.

Proceeding incrementally carries an interactive benefit when the patient is a mental health professional. Regardless of which modality is chosen, this way of proceeding gives a higher prestige to, and hence allows the mental health professional to feel better about, practicing psychotherapy. Such an interactive benefit must become a focus of investigation if the psychoanalytically oriented psychotherapy or the psychoanalysis is to maintain its psychoanalytic orientation. It is striking how embedded in such professional considerations are fragile and otherwise compromised self-esteem and self-concepts, competitive conflicts, and the like, which are easily overlooked if one becomes procedural regarding the modalities.

This incremental manner of proceeding may give too much weight to the patient's choice. Yet if an error is to be made, it is better to err on that side. In practice, this manner of proceeding becomes a dialectic of the patient's and the psychotherapist's contributions and evolves out of progressive understanding. This approach stands in marked contrast to a method recommended by many psychoanalysts—evaluation followed by presentation of "the treatment of choice." Presentation of the treatment of choice emphasizes "procedure" and "therapy" and uses the transference too much in the effort to be psychoanalytic (Fisher, 1987). "The treatment of choice" method also leaves the patient and the psychotherapist with the problem of first- and second-class psychotherapies and what to do when the preferred "choice" is not possible.

It is of interest that in the 1983 panel of the American Psychoanalytic Association on conversion of psychotherapy to psychoanalysis, it was evident that many psychoanalysts proceed in this incremental manner using psychotherapy as a valued procedure for evaluating analyzability and as a way of working through many of the resistances to psychoanalysis (cited in Fisher, 1987). In the panel and floor discussion, there was strong support for the compatibility of psychotherapy with subsequent psychoanalysis by the same practitioner when the psychotherapy was not overly interactive or manipulative. Latent in the discussion was a strong dichotomy between psychoanalytically oriented and interactive psychotherapy, not so labeled.

A DOUBLE HELIX: A CONCEPTUAL MODEL

Psychoanalysis evolved from, and developed in contrast to, hypnosis. Although arising within a medical tradition and using a medical lexicon, psychoanalysis early recognized that its scope was beyond the therapeutic (Freud, 1926).

As psychoanalysis wrestled with the relation of suggestion to interpretation, the bimodal model of hypnosis and psychoanalysis permeated the early discussions. With the development of a psychotherapeutic enterprise, the bimodal model blended into bipartite procedures, psychotherapy and psychoanalysis. As understanding of the processes within the procedures became more sophisticated, there evolved within the bimodal model an intermediate form variously called psychoanalytic psychotherapy, psychoanalytically oriented psychotherapy, and exploratory psychotherapy. As theories of technique developed, the way the modalities were regarded varied depending on emphasis. Currently, most theoreticians and clinicians use a continuum model within the tripartite division, a position championed by no less a theoretician and researcher than Robert Wallerstein (1986).

Gill's (1982) stunning recanting of his 1954 classical paper, which defined psychoanalysis and the tripartite division for the large body of psychoanalytic practitioners, reestablished a bimodal model. In this model, Gill identified transferential interpretive intervention as the characteristic of psychoanalysis; he relegated frequency and use of the couch to less importance and sharply separated psychoanalysis from psychotherapy.

Building on Gill's later paradigm, I propose a bimodal model regarding predominant intervention (mode), interactive versus interpretive modes, while maintaining a tripartite division of procedure (modality). In my tripartite division, the modalities become *interactive psychotherapy,* and the two interpretive psychotherapies, *psychoanalytically oriented psychotherapy* and *psychoanalysis.*

In this model, the three modalities are not on a continuum nor are they equidistant from each other, nor is the relationship among them considered only in a linear plane. Although all three share commonalities, the distance between interactive psychotherapy and the two interpretive psychotherapies, psychoanalytically oriented psychotherapy and psychoanalysis, is greater for critical variables than is the distance between psychoanalytically oriented psychotherapy and psychoanalysis. When viewed as processes, interactive psychotherapy also stands relatively alone, whereas psychoanalytically oriented psychotherapy and psychoanalysis are intrinsically and complexly interrelated. Visually, psychoanalytically oriented psychotherapy and psychoanalysis become a double helix, entwined yet distinct.

The three-dimensional image of the double helix allows a visible representation of psychoanalytically oriented psychotherapy and psychoanalysis as intertwining, complementary processes with intersections often more apparent than real. In short, although having components in common, psychoanalytically oriented psychotherapy and psychoanalysis as modalities seem more nearly identical than they are.

CHAPTER 9

In Summary

The purpose of this book is to define a psychotherapy that is based on the psychoanalytic theory of psychodynamics and development *and* on the technique of psychoanalysis. The term psychoanalytically oriented psychotherapy, more precisely defined, is revived to emphasize that the orientation of the psychotherapy (not just of the psychotherapist) is psychoanalytic. A new, triadic nomenclature for the psychotherapies is offered: interactive psychotherapy, psychoanalytically oriented psychotherapy, and psychoanalysis.

Interactive psychotherapy is psychotherapy whose mode uses transference in directive, suggestive, and manipulative interventions, with modeling and *selective* transference interpretation, to produce changes largely according to the psychotherapist's evaluation. If the psychotherapist is psychoanalytically oriented, the interventions will be psychoanalytically guided. The prototype of the interactive psychotherapist is the seer/hypnotist. Although broadly effective therapeutically, interactive psychotherapy essentially directs, and therefore limits, understanding.

Psychoanalytically oriented psychotherapy and psychoanalysis are interpretive in mode. Although interpretation is an interaction, as an intervention it is qualitatively different from any other intervention in that interpretation attempts to add explicit knowledge and when transferential makes the interaction itself the object of analysis.

The interplay in psychoanalytically oriented psychotherapy and psychoanalysis can be characterized along innumerable axes with each modality having specifics that move the material in different directions. Within the external dialogue of the psychotherapeutic exchange in both psychoanalytically oriented psychotherapy and psychoanalysis is a specific kind of internal soliloquy, a complex intrapsychic "conversation" between longitudinal and cross-sectional aspects of the self with various externalizations and displacements interacting with and being organized by the external dialogue.

"The couch" *symbolizes* the difference between psychoanalysis and psychoanalytically oriented psychotherapy. The couch in psychoanalysis is a shorthand designation for a kind of external dialogue, when the frequency of sessions is sufficient, in which there is contrived lessening of the dynamic, ongoing verbal and nonverbal negotiations in communication that characterize the face-to-face interchange of psychoanalytically oriented psychotherapy. In psychoanalytically oriented psychotherapy, the internal soliloquy remains more strongly *within* the external dialogue than it does in psychoanalysis.

Both psychoanalytically oriented psychotherapy and psychoanalysis have extensive aims. Yet each modality explores different areas of the interplay. Both provide Freud's "after-education"— new perspectives gained through emotional reevaluation, reliving, and vitalized insight—with differing potentials and limitations. In broad sweeps, the after-education of psychoanalytically oriented psychotherapy is cross-sectional; that is, the interplay emphasizes the psychodynamics of interpersonal functioning with correspondingly less detailed, genetic detailing. The after-education of psychoanalysis carries a longitudinal emphasis; that is, the interplay is heavily laced with genetically detailed reconstruction and less detailing of the psychodynamics of the ongoing interpersonal functioning. The prototype of the psychoanalytically oriented psychotherapist and the psychoanalyst is the teacher in its broadest meaning.

Although there is considerable overlap and variation depending on the psychotherapeutic dyad, in general the nature of the modalities dictate this bimodal quality. For the patient suitable for either modality, an empirical determination of which aftereducation provides more is yet to come, even though experience suggests that, from the clinically therapeutic perspective, the procedures roughly are equally effective.

Underlying this conceptual triadic schema of the psychotherapies resides a bimodal epistemological construct. The therapeutic orientation of psychotherapy has its origins in the social sciences. This therapeutic orientation derives from the turn of the century's optimistic application of science to the humanities to *better* humankind's lot. The aftereducations of psychoanalysis and psychoanalytically oriented psychotherapy are part of an older tradition, a continuation of humankind's attempt to *understand* itself better.

Yet, depending on vantage point, psychoanalytically oriented psychotherapy and psychoanalysis, sometimes actually, but more often only seemingly, intersect. Their historical affiliations and separatenesses, essential commonalities and distinct manifestations, and component alignments and component differences, entwined and yet fully distinct, evoke the spatial image of the double helix. As spiraling complementary lines of pursuit, psychoanalytically oriented psychotherapy and psychoanalysis are part of a mighty armamentarium in humankind's quest for self-knowledge and self-potentiation—a double helix of humanism in the pure sense.

CHAPTER 10

Indirect Suggestion: A Response to Oremland's *Interpretation and Interaction*

Merton M. Gill

Freud's remarks on the distinction between psychoanalysis and psychotherapy, as we now make it, were very few. Probably the best known is this: ". . . the large-scale application of our therapy will compel us to alloy the pure gold of analysis freely with the copper of *direct* suggestion . . . (1919, p. 168, italics added). Since Freud, the distinction has become ever more important. It carries powerful emotional freight. Those who *seem* to minimize the distinction are often considered not really to understand analysis. This monograph (and my chapter, I hope) will sharpen rather than blur the distinction by focusing on *indirect* suggestion. Of course, it must be remembered that the definitions of psychoanalysis and psychotherapy were not handed down with the tablets of the law. They are man made.

When I received Jerome Oremland's manuscript, I quickly became fascinated with it. So many of his ideas on the relationship of psychoanalysis to psychotherapy, and indeed the major thrust of his presentation, were like mine, which I had come to regard as relatively idiosyncratic. It was clear that although he referred liberally to my work—though not as much to recent changes in my thinking (Gill, 1982, 1984a, b) as I would have liked—he had arrived at his views independently of me. It also was apparent that he, more

---

I owe much to my continuing conversations with Irwin Z. Hoffman.

extensively than I, had implemented the viewpoint we both espouse. This disparity derives from the fact that my ideas in this area
were consolidated relatively late in my career, by which time I was
practicing relatively little psychotherapy. I have continued, be it
noted, to do a good deal of psychotherapy supervision.

After I sent Dr. Oremland an extensive critique, he generously
invited me to join him in his project. At first I was reluctant to do
more than provide an endorsement. It seemed unfair to ride piggy
back on his work, nor did I want to imply a blanket endorsement of
all his interesting ideas. Later I concluded that I was more likely
reluctant simply to append myself to a book that, in many ways,
resembled the one I might have written. I also sought a greater
currency for certain revisions of my ideas, as noted earlier. So I
agreed to write a concluding chapter, which the author of this work
would be free to accept or reject. Happily he has accepted it.

What I have written must be read not in the context of my
claiming more or even equal experience, but, rather, in the light of
my extrapolation from the experience I have. I say "extrapolate"
because I have not used the technique Oremland and I describe in
lengthy therapies, as he has. He has applied this technique in
long-term therapy with an ambitious aim, whereas I, while not
disputing such applicability, have myself employed it only in
briefer therapies of varying duration. I have, however, conducted
weekly seminars for 10 years in which the participants present three
consecutive audio-recorded sessions from therapies that are often
lengthy. The sessions are discussed in terms of the model presented
here.

Let me state our primary agreement and difference at the outset.
Our agreement is that there is a central distinction to be made in the
techniques of psychological therapy. As Oremland says, the distinction is between interaction with analysis of the interaction and
interaction without analysis of the interaction. It is unfortunately
easy to fall into a very misleading shorthand and speak of a dichotomy between interaction and interpretation or between interaction and analysis of interaction. Such a shorthand risks abetting
the serious error of forgetting that all interventions are interactions,
including interventions that aim to analyze interaction. Note that
the title of the monograph is "Interaction *and* Interpretation," not
"Interaction *or* Interpretation."

To adopt the latter formulation, thereby juxtaposing interaction and interpretation, would be to imply a sharper dichotomy than is connoted by the distinction between interaction *with* analysis of the interaction and interaction *without* analysis of the interaction. The interactive effect of the analysis of an interaction can be more important than the effect of the original interaction.

Oremland and I likewise agree that this latter distinction is a key factor in differentiating psychotherapy from psychoanalysis as an ideal, psychoanalysis being characterized aphoristically as interaction with analysis of interaction and psychotherapy as interaction without analysis of interaction. Our agreement is reflected in the fact that Oremland discusses in detail many interactions with patients, both nonverbal and verbal, that are often taken for granted and left unanalyzed. I suspect that such interactions find their way into conversations among therapists more often than in the literature.

It may be that "interaction" is too pallid a term. For me at least, it need not connote the kind of affective interpersonal influence I have in mind. The distinction we are making is more usually cast as the manipulation of the transference versus the analysis of the transference. Manipulation of the transference is often called suggestion.

Another important aspect of the aforementioned distinction is whether the interaction in question is witting or not. Since every intervention, indeed the therapy situation itself, is an interaction, it is always witting in that sense. But an important distinction must be drawn between an interaction that is designed to have an interpersonal effect and an interaction that has such an effect but was not intended to do so.

The latter distinction is an aspect of an important disagreement between Oremland and me. It concerns what he regards as an important epistemological distinction between psychotherapy and psychoanalysis. He regards the former as inextricably limited and limiting, even though ameliorating and therapeutic, and the latter as potentially expanding because of its emphasis on increasing understanding and insight, Freud's after-education. He says that "interpretation as an intervention is qualitatively different from other interactions in that its aim is solely to add explicit knowledge . . . whereas interactive interventions remain largely experiential (p. 10)." I agree with this distinction, but I also believe that whereas the interpersonal effect of an interpretation may be unwitting in the immediate context of the single interpretation, *one* of the central aims of all psychological therapy, including psychoanalysis, is to bring about an interpersonal effect. Such an effect inheres in the situation of psychological therapy; it will come about regardless of the therapist's conscious intent.

I realize that I am touching on the issue of whether change comes about by way of insight or by way of the relationship. I consider the dichotomy false: these two possibilities can only be conceptually separated, although in any particular analysis one or the other may seem preponderant. I believe Oremland's view is a remnant of the classical idea that lasting change comes about only through understanding; I believe, furthermore, that this view is part of a "one-person" conception of psychoanalysis, which is mistaken, because, as I said, the psychoanalytic situation is inherently interpersonal.[2]

There is another, albeit less important, way in which Oremland and I differ: Oremland is convinced that the couch and the greater frequency of visits in analysis necessarily result in a major emphasis on reconstruction; whereas the face-to-face posture and lesser frequency of visits in therapy necessarily result in a major emphasis on the patient–therapist interaction, although he grants that there is major overlap in the two therapy situations. I believe the distinction may be due to the therapist's behavior and inclinations and that the question is yet to be resolved by research.

A NEW PARADIGM

I believe that Oremland's study needs to be placed in a wider context. His organizing focus is the relationship between psychoanalysis and psychotherapy. Mine has primarily been the theory

---

[2]I discovered recently, to my astonishment, that some analysts believe "interpersonal" means what actually takes place between analyst and analysand in contrast to "intrapsychic," which means how what takes place is experienced by the analysand. It is almost beyond my comprehension how any analyst can believe that another analyst makes such a distinction. I say "almost" because it must mean that some analysts believe they *know* what actually goes on, while the patient has only a particular (and allegedly often distorted) *experience* of what went on.

and the analysis of transference, although I have also written (1984b) with a focus on psychoanalysis and psychotherapy. But I believe the context needs to be broadened to what I (1984a) have called a new paradigm for psychoanalysis. "New paradigm" is a somewhat misleading term because it neglects the work of precursors, yet it is indeed only recently that the paradigm has become fully explicit. It has two facets aptly named social-constructivist by Irwin Z. Hoffman (in press). Social refers both to the therapist's involvement and to the fact that each of the two participants in any therapy shapes the other. Constructivist refers to the fact that each participant "reads" the other from his own perspective. Constructivist might, by itself, denote how each participant shapes the other, in which case the paradigm could simply be called the constructivist paradigm; but the latter term is usually used only to refer to how one reads a "text." The social aspect of the paradigm is by far the older. Ferenczi (1925), Sullivan (1953), Balint (1965), and Racker (1968) were prominent in recognizing the analyst's participation, but they emphasized primarily the social, and not the constructivist, aspect of the paradigm.[3] Schafer (1983) more recently has emphasized primarily a constructionist but not a social paradigm.[4]

Today the development of the paradigm is being carried forward by Hoffman and a group from the William Alanson White Institute among others. Much of their work has been published in the journal *Contemporary Psychoanalysis*. Many people erroneously believe that the constructivist paradigm rejects psychosexuality and intrapsychic organization. Although the paradigm has frequently been used without those two staples of psychoanalysis, it need not be.

In Wallerstein's (1984) friendly critique of my 1982 monograph on transference, he tried to save me from what he felt was my implication that I was proposing a new paradigm. I (1984a) replied that I was doing just that in redefining transference. I should have

---

[3]A rereading of Racker's book (1968) reminds me that although he writes in a Kleinian idiom, and although he does not deal with the relationship between psychoanalysis and psychotherapy, many of the ideas in this book and in my chapter—particularly the relationship between interaction and interpretation—are already there.

[4]Hoffman (1990, personal communication) suggests that the division into two facets is misleading in that a participant paradigm necessarily implies a constructivist one, and vice versa.

made more clear that the central issue was not my emphasis on the analysis of transference, but on the redefinition of transference. In fact, the redefinition of transference arises from a more basic redefinition of the analytic situation as social-constructivist, but I did not fully realize that then. *It would be an error to read Oremland's monograph as a brief for the employment of the usual analytic technique but at lesser frequency and sitting up. His major thesis is, rather, that with the recognition of the social nature of the analytic situation the issues of the ubiquity of interaction and the distinction between interaction with and without the analysis of interaction become central.*

TERMINOLOGY

The issue of nomenclature is important and potentially confusing. Oremland does not distinguish sharply enough between what psychotherapists are doing and what he would like them to do. He would like a tripartite distinction among interactive psychotherapy, psychoanalytically oriented psychotherapy, and psychoanalysis. But what is called psychoanalytically oriented psychotherapy, or, equivalently and more frequently, called psychoanalytic psychotherapy, is very different from what Oremland calls psychoanalytically oriented psychotherapy. Actually, most currently practiced psychotherapy exists on a continuum with supportive psychotherapy at one pole—a variety of Oremland's interactive psychotherapy—and at the other pole a psychotherapy in which the analysis of transference plays a central role, even though significant unanalyzed transferences are wittingly left unanalyzed.[5] The continuum proceeds from the supportive pole through progressively diminishing unanalyzed interaction and progressively increasing analysis of transference (and the other features of psychoanalysis), to the pole of little (witting) unanalyzed interaction and predominant analysis of transference (and the other features of psychoanalysis). In my paper of 1954 I designated this entire continuum (minus

---

[5]In most of these, analysis of transference means noting, at best, parallels between earlier experience and the way the therapist believes the patient is experiencing the interaction.

the solely interactive pole, which I called "supportive psychotherapy") "exploratory psychotherapy." It is at the analytic pole that
exploratory psychotherapy shades into what Oremland calls psychoanalytically oriented psychotherapy. I called the middle range of
the continuum the "intermediate" form of psychotherapy. What
Oremland calls "interactive" and "analytic" I termed, respectively,
"supportive" and "exploratory."

I believe that, among practitioners, psychoanalytically oriented
psychotherapy usually denotes the continuum encompassed by my
term exploratory psychotherapy. Oremland disagrees, believing
rather that that was more common at one time, but that now
psychoanalytic psychotherapy is the usual term for the continuum.
Indeed it is because he considers psychoanalytically oriented psychotherapy a relatively little-used term that he considers it available
for the therapy he describes in this book. I believe both terms are
commonly taken to represent the continuum, even if the one term is
used less frequently than the other. I do not know how many people
practice what Oremland calls psychoanalytically oriented psychotherapy; I believe not many. On the other hand, I suspect many
practice toward the psychoanalytic pole of the continuum I term
exploratory psychotherapy, whether or not they are psychoanalysts.

I do not like the term "psychoanalytically oriented psychotherapy" for what Oremland describes because it implies too great a gap
between psychoanalysis and the modality he describes. Oremland,
for his part, criticizes the revision of my ideas published in 1984
because he feels I make the gap between the two modalities too
narrow. Perhaps Oremland wants to retain the term psychotherapy
as part of the name of the new modality he is endorsing because he
wants to distinguish it quite sharply from psychoanalysis. But
"psychotherapy" usually has the connotation of a mixture of analyzed and unanalyzed interaction, and this mixture is not what
Oremland means to convey. He says that in speaking of psychoanalytically oriented psychotherapy *he is referring to the orientation of the
therapy* as well as the therapist, but I do not see that this clarification
answers my objections to the term.

I (Gill, 1984b) also proposed a tripartite distinction between (a)
interactive psychotherapy (although I did not use this term and it was
more implicit than explicit in my discussion); (b) what I hesitantly

called *psychoanalytic technique* (which, as I will describe later, is in some ways like and in some ways unlike Oremland's psychoanalytically oriented psychotherapy); and (c) *psychoanalysis.*

I should point out that both Oremland and I are omitting a significant part of what actually goes on in the field, namely that part of the continuum in which there is a good deal of analysis of interaction but that is not yet what we are denoting by the adjective "psychoanalytic." What are we to call a therapy in which there is a relatively small but significant amount of intentionally unanalyzed interaction? It does not qualify as either Oremland's psychoanalytically oriented psychotherapy or as psychoanalysis proper because of the intentionally unanalyzed interaction. It is somewhere on the continuum. So we really need four terms: interactive psychotherapy, intermediate psychotherapy, psychoanalytically oriented psychotherapy (if we accept Oremland's term), and psychoanalysis proper. I will return to the bothersome issue of terminology later.

Oremland believes that my use of the label "psychoanalytic technique" signifies a failure to distinguish adequately between what I called psychoanalytic technique—which, to repeat, is in some respects like and in some respects different from his psychoanalytically oriented psychotherapy—and psychoanalysis. I see the fault of the term "psychoanalytic technique"; this term commonly refers to a mode, whereas I was describing a modality, a distinction to which I now turn.

MODE AND MODALITY

Oremland very usefully introduces these terms into his discussion. It was in preparing my (in press) reply to Wallerstein's (1989; in press) misunderstanding of my point of view that I first became clearly aware of how the concepts "mode" and "modality" could be used to clarify discussions of psychoanalysis and psychotherapy.

Bibring (1954) first defined the difference between techniques he described five: suggestion, abreaction, manipulation, clarification, and interpretation—and methods, such as dynamic psychotherapy, nondirective (Rogerian) therapy, and psychoanalysis. Bibring suggested that methods were made up of various combinations of techniques. Oremland is suggesting "mode" as an alternate term for technique and "modality" as an alternate term for method.

Bibring was of the opinion that all the techniques were used in a psychoanalysis, but he did not emphasize as strongly as Oremland and I that, although all the techniques are used, the aim of analysis is to analyze their interactive meanings. Wallerstein (1989) and Rangell (1981) see the presence of techniques other than interpretation as "infiltrations" into analysis, whether advertent or inadvertent, rather than as intrinsic aspects of a therapeutic situation, that is, by definition, an interpersonal interaction. Every intervention, indeed the therapeutic situation itself, has interactional, that is, suggestive, meaning. If the therapy is to be an analysis these suggestive implications must be made as explicit as possible; that is, their implicit, unreflected upon influence must be made explicit. My point here is related to the one that Eissler (1953) made in describing deviations (parameters) from analysis. He insisted that for a method to be analytic these parameters had to be "resolved" by interpretation.

The difference between Eissler's view and the view that Oremland and I espouse is that, for Eissler, a parameter was usually a single, gross suggestion, like advising the analysand against getting married; whereas for Oremland and me the entire analytic situation is shot through with suggestion, whether witting or unwitting, that should be made as explicit as possible. We speak of the ubiquity of interaction.

The following quotations from Wallerstein and Rangell will illustrate my claim that they do not recognize that any therapy situation, including the psychoanalytic one, is an interpersonal interaction with suggestive meaning:

> . . . and this is the major understanding of the results of the Menninger project—inevitable infiltrations, advertent or inadvertent, of admixtures of more supportive techniques and modes into even the efforts at the purest of expressive-analytic approaches [psychoanalysis] [Wallerstein, 1989, p. 588].

> There is no analysis without its share of the technical maneuvers noted by Bibring (1954) . . . which are not inadvertent but built-in and by design. Nor are they of themselves necessarily parameters but accessory and preparatory modes intrinsic to the treatment [Rangell, 1981, p. 585].

Obviously Wallerstein and Rangell are thoroughly conversant with the ideas of Bibring and Eissler, but they do not see the ubiquity of interaction and the need to make it explicit if the therapy is to be psychoanalytic, the critical technical thesis of Oremland's book. As a result they blur the distinction between psychotherapy and psychoanalysis. Yes, interaction is inevitable in psychoanalysis, but, unlike psychotherapy, the aim is to make it explicit. Analysts customarily speak of the need to "resolve" it, but this term is vague. Does it mean to completely nullify the effect? To nullify only some aspects of it? If the latter, then which aspects? Does it refer to the elimination of repetitive, neurotic interpersonal patterns or more benign patterns as well?

PSYCHOANALYTICALLY ORIENTED PSYCHOTHERAPY VERSUS PSYCHOANALYSIS

I wonder whether the difference Oremland finds between psychoanalysis and his psychoanalytically oriented psychotherapy is iatrogenic or intrinsic. I say I "wonder" because I do not have adequate first-hand experience to come down on one side or the other. My skepticism about the difference does reflect 10 years of experience in the weekly seminar, mentioned earlier, in which the participants present, in turn, three consecutive audio-recorded sessions of lengthy therapies, most of which were carried out at a frequency of only once a week and all of which were face to face.

The issue has to do with the difference between face-to-face therapy of less than three or four times a week on one hand, and the use of the couch at a frequency of at least three times a week on the other, even when psychoanalytic technique is used in both circumstances.[6] Oremland, acknowledging that there can be considerable overlap, argues that in the first situation there is inevitably greater attention to the nuances of the here-and-now relationship between patient and therapist, whereas in the second situation there is inevitably greater attention to the development of the narrative of

---

[6]Five-times-a-week, face-to-face therapy is usually used with people not considered "analyzable," although Oremland apparently finds that in some instances even with severely disturbed individuals, he can carry out his psychoanalytically oriented psychotherapy that way.

the illness. While there may be spontaneous tendencies in these directions, I suggest, and Oremland agrees, that in a particular situation, though the external circumstances influence how the transference develops, the very reverse of Oremland's contention may be the case. On one hand, in face-to-face therapy, if one is indeed analyzing the transference, there may be a greater temptation to skirt the more intensely affect-laden erotic and aggressive interaction. On the other hand, with the use of the couch, the therapist may feel freer to tackle these more intense erotic and aggressive interactions because they seem less "personal." The same can be said with respect to the issue of frequency. With less frequent visits the therapist may hesitate to open "hot" interpersonal issues, whereas with more frequent sessions he may feel able to do so. Generalizations in these matters are not possible. What happens depends on the particular analyst–analysand pair. It may be that as our training psychoanalyses and training psychoanalytically oriented psychotherapies (to use Oremland's distinction) become more adequate, our countertransferences will be less inhibiting to our dealing openly with these more profound interactions. Or is this a counsel of perfection?

Oremland has suggested in our discussions that I underestimate the significance of the couch and frequency of sessions in determining the material. I ask whether assuming that the couch—or any other aspect of the therapeutic situation—has the same meaning to all patients and therapists is not a violation of his own principle. To assume that the meaning of the couch can be understood without making explicit its meaning for a particular patient–therapist pair is to reject the need to analyze an interaction. *To regard the couch as having a universal meaning is psychotherapeutic, but to examine its various meanings to various patients and therapists is psychoanalytic.* Although I am sure Oremland endorses analysis of the meaning of the couch and frequency of sessions, the significance he attaches to them seems contradictory to the distinction between unanalyzed interaction and analyzed interaction. For many patients—and for many therapists—there are doubtless powerful differences in the meaning of the couch and the frequency of sessions. And it is impossible to generalize about the degree to which the thorough explication of the meanings of couch and frequency of sessions will affect the process; but it is important not to slide into the error of ascribing universality to one a priori interpretation at the expense of the range of potential meanings. Of course, the meaning of position has to take account of the position in which it is explored.

Oremland sharply opposes the use of the couch in his psychoanalytically oriented psychotherapy. He suggests that when it is so used the therapist may on occasion be claiming the prestige of psychoanalysis when he is not qualified to do so. I would reply that when this is the case, there is presumably a falseness about the therapy that is hardly likely to be combined with a careful analysis of the transference-countertransference meaning of the couch. I hold that there may be circumstances in which the couch would be helpful in his psychoanalytically oriented psychotherapy, whereas Oremland justifiably feels that such use is likely to be an unanalyzed interaction. The use of the couch for prestige is, of course, but one of the important social meanings that can play a role in the definition and practice of psychoanalysis and psychotherapy. Oremland touches on such meanings here and there and would no doubt agree that they are worthy of more extended consideration.

Oremland is opposed to the use of the instruction to free associate not only in psychoanalytically oriented psychotherapy but in psychoanalysis as well. I believe its aim should be sought and that, if used, its suggestive effect must be analyzed.

I was struck by the fact that Oremland's illustrations of analyzed interactions were mainly in the context of his psychoanalytically oriented psychotherapy rather than psychoanalysis. Although he claims that these examples are equally applicable to analysis, this is perhaps another indication of his conviction that interpersonal interaction inevitably plays a greater role in the former modality than in the latter. On the other hand, it may be that his examples were drawn from psychoanalytically oriented psychotherapy because his primary focus in this book is on defining this modality and its relation to psychoanalysis.

With Oremland, I suggest that the usual beginning of a psychoanalysis with an implied aim and duration is a major and, I suspect, frequently unanalyzed interaction. The notion of a psychological therapy without mutually significant interaction between the two participants is nonsense, because psychological therapy is an affect-laden situation. But is it not preferable to avoid unnecessary witting interaction, especially if such interaction tends to slip away unnoticed? Or does this idea of avoiding unnecessary witting activity itself imply an unanalyzed interaction? Indeed, are any quantitative formulations, such as more or less activity, a lapse from dealing with meanings? Again, with Oremland, I suggest an *incremental* way of doing his psychoanalytically oriented psychotherapy; *but, more radically, I believe it should be considered for what could become an analysis with couch and frequent sessions too.* As the expert, the therapist should make suggestions for the beginning extrinsic arrangements, but they should be mutually determined with major leeway to the patient. Then changes in the extrinsic arrangements should flow from the material and be joint decisions, especially carefully analyzed (Gill, 1988). With the incremental approach, the distinction between Oremland's psychoanalytically oriented psychotherapy and psychoanalysis lessens and perhaps even disappears, a view Oremland does not share because he believes that the axis of the material is *necessarily* more affected by couch and frequency of sessions than I do.

Oremland believes that his psychoanalytically oriented psychotherapy has wider application than classical psychoanalysis, that it is employable with some character disorders, borderline states, and even psychoses for which classical analysis has traditionally been deemed inapplicable. Why the difference? I agree that something other than nosology is involved. Could it be something interactive? I (1984b) have suggested that for some patients the couch and frequent sessions may be a powerful support, while for others they may mean a terrifying, relentless pursuit. Some severely disturbed patients for whom the couch and frequent visits are intolerably invasive may be able to tolerate and benefit from analytic work in the context of less frequent face-to-face therapy. Oremland correctly sees that in an analytic psychotherapy such meanings would be exposed and explored.

It may be that some of the differences Oremland cites between the two modalities are not only a function of a failure to make the meaning of the extrinsic factors adequately explicit, as I have been arguing, but perhaps even more likely a function of different kinds of patients. Is it not true that sicker patients often refuse to be good (docile) patients and that they force difficult transference issues early and explicitly? Oremland's rejoinder is that whereas the difference between the two modalities may be enhanced by their use with different kinds of patients, the distinction between the two modalities holds for patients for whom psychoanalytically oriented psychotherapy and psychoanalysis are equally applicable.

PSYCHOANALYTICALLY ORIENTED PSYCHOTHERAPY VERSUS PSYCHOANALYTIC TECHNIQUE

When I wrote about "analytic technique" (1984b) I meant something different from Oremland's "psychoanalytically oriented psychotherapy." I did not rule out a therapy with as ambitious an aim as psychoanalysis purports to have and a duration as long as that of psychoanalysis, although I was not explicit about it. I implied a therapy that would go on only as long as circumstances warranted and until the two participants decided it should end. I suggested, on the basis of experience, that such a therapy could be interrupted without harm and without the loss of what had been gained. I implied, further, that such a therapy could be time limited with a prior agreement as to its duration. Such an agreement would, of course, be a major interactive move, but that interaction itself would be a major focus of interpretation. Mann's (1973) time-limited psychotherapy is an example of how such an initial interaction shapes the therapy and is interpreted.

I do not argue against Oremland's psychoanalytically oriented psychotherapy. But I do ask whether analytic technique, as I use the term, may not have broader application than he considers. Although Oremland believes that I do not distinguish sharply enough between psychoanalysis proper and psychoanalytic technique with altered extrinsic criteria, he too can be read to be narrowing the gap between his psychoanalytically oriented psychotherapy and psychoanalysis. He says the two modalities share the same ambitious aim and the same duration, although psychoanalytically oriented psychotherapy dispenses with the couch and requires less frequent sessions. Even if one were to grant him the difference in emphasis between the here-and-now and reconstruction of the past associated with the two variants, is Oremland not in essence arguing that a *psychoanalysis* can be effectively carried out without the couch and at a lesser frequency? Oremland believes that in saying this I am blurring what he regards as two distinct modalities.

What is the lower limit of frequency at which psychoanalytic technique can be used? I don't know. The answer depends a great deal on the particular patient-therapist couple. I believe that psychoanalysis can sometimes be done once a week. There seems to be a general feeling among therapists that the change from once to twice a week is much greater than from twice a week to more. Freud (1913) said that "for slight cases or the continuation of a treatment which is already well advanced, three days a week will be enough" (p. 127). On the other hand, some analysts place enough importance on daily sessions to speak of the "Monday crust."

Oremland and I propose the same essential distinction: interaction with and without its analysis. The difference between my "analytic technique" and his "psychoanalytically oriented psychotherapy" is unrelated to this distinction since both notions are *modally* the same—both require analysis of interaction as opposed to interaction without its analysis—even though they represent different *modalities*.

I repeat that the distinction between interaction with and without its analysis can be mistakenly read to imply that there can be analysis, whether of interaction or otherwise, that is not itself an interaction or a therapy in which all interaction has been made explicit. Both ideas are nonsense. Everything in the therapeutic process has interactive meaning. The analysis of an interaction is also an interaction. It is not possible to bring interaction to an end by analyzing it; it can only be increased in awareness, better understood, and at times modified. Here Oremland and I are in full agreement.

In the therapy Oremland and I endorse, the aim is to analyze the interaction to the greatest extent possible. Limits are set by the patient's and the psychotherapist's personalities as well as by the psychotherapist's skill. We agree that the patient's diagnostic category is often not the relevant variable. Further, I do not believe it possible to tell beforehand or even early on whether a patient is amenable to analysis of the interaction. Such analysis may be possible only later on, sometimes much later on, and with regard to certain issues and not others. There may be particular issues with respect to which the interaction seems thoroughly clear to the psychotherapist but the patient rejects any attempt to make it explicit.

The patient's reaction to the interpretation of interaction may take the form of accusing the analyst of being too preoccupied with the interaction between himself and the patient. Indeed it is not only the patient who may ask, "Why do you think everything has to do with you?" It has been suggested (Blum, 1983, p. 615) that a psychotherapy that emphasizes the analysis of the here-and-now degenerates into a narcissistic preoccupation with the psychotherapist at the expense of the patient. It can, but that does not mean it must or even that it often does. It is true that attentiveness to the here-and-now interaction, with its concomitant loosening of the restraints typified by the caricature of the silent analyst, has its dangers. But the silent analyst is also engaged in an interaction—an interaction that he is not likely to recognize he is contributing to and therefore not likely to analyze.

What makes a therapy analytic is not the immediate and insistent interpretation of everything in the process that can be construed as having a transference implication. That would in itself constitute a major, undesirable, and likely unanalyzable interaction. Some of my previous writings on the subject are open to that charge. Even some aspects of this essay could be thus misconstrued. What makes a therapy analytic is the analyst's conviction of the value of such interpretation and his attempt to carry it out as fully as possible within the context of the patient's material and his own capacities. On the other side, it must be stated that just as the therapist can be too eager to make such interpretations, so he can be overly reluctant, invoking all manner of rationalizations. Oremland's study is a beginning investigation of what makes a situation "right" or "not right" for the analysis of interaction. Transference analysis is likely to be the most difficult aspect of psychological therapy for the analyst as well as the patient.

REGRESSION

The matter of regression in the therapeutic situation is an important issue to which Oremland has failed to give adequate attention. I have earlier (1984b) distinguished between two views of couch and frequency of sessions in relation to regression. If regression is considered an essential feature of the psychoanalytic process and if couch and frequency of sessions are considered essential to bringing about regression, then couch and frequency are no longer dispensable extrinsic factors in the psychoanalytic process. If, on the other hand, regression is not an essential feature of the psychoanalytic process, or if regression will take place even without couch and sufficiently frequent sessions, then couch and frequency are indeed extrinsic factors in the sense that they are not intrinsic to the establishment of a psychoanalytic situation.

There is a major inconsistency in classical analytic writing on regression. On one hand, regression is regarded as a spontaneous development, and, on the other, it is regarded as brought about by the couch and frequency of sessions. If the latter is true, is it not iatrogenic? (Bear in mind that iatrogenic does not mean that the analyst alone is responsible.) As I have noted (Gill, 1984b), Macalpine's (1950) often-quoted paper regards the analytic process as a slowly carried out hypnotic induction. I suggest that classical analysis blinds itself to this inconsistency by attributing the regression to the setting and not to the analyst, who, after all, is responsible for the setting. Oremland too speaks of regression as having an "iatrogenic quality." I presume he means that, like all transference, it is contributed to by both participants with the psychoanalyst's contribution varying from a minor to a major one.

Roy Schafer (1985) has criticized me for claiming that the psychoanalytic setting infantilizes the patient. He believes that if the patient experiences the setting as infantilizing, this is the result of the patient's personality. In a way he is right. If I insist that the setting is infantilizing, I am saying that it inevitably has this effect. Yet I have just argued that the couch and frequency of sessions can mean different things to different people. In another way Schafer is wrong. The classical psychoanalyst arranges this setting in order to "induce" regression to the infantile neurosis; in this sense he attempts to infantilize the patient. Of course, a patient may not become infantilized even if he is on the couch and coming frequently. But is he not then considered to be resisting or even to be unanalyzable?

The analyst wants the regression, if such it is, to be confined to the psychoanalytic situation—a regression in the service of the ego (Kris, 1952). But what exactly are the phenomena that are regarded as regressive? Whatever they are, Oremland suggests that instead of calling them a transference neurosis we should call them "regressive transference enactment" (p. 36). In making this suggestion he is proposing that enactment is a necessary part of a transference neurosis. The point is the same as Freud's (1914) distinction between repeating and remembering: enactment is regressive as compared with remembering.

Oremland quotes an arresting statement by Arlow (1975) on regression: ". . . what the psychoanalytic situation does is to create an atmosphere, a set of conditions, which permit regressive aspects of the patient's mental functioning, long present, to reemerge in forms that are clearer and easier to observe" (p. 73). In my paper of 1984b, in which I cited the same passage, I wrote: "I would differ only in that I would say that what Arlow describes is what analysis *should* aim for but that the usual analytic setting and practice may well often induce an additional unnecessary, if not harmful, iatrogenic regression" (p. 170). Stone (1961) made an early contribution to our understanding of such unnecessary iatrogenic regression.

But if "regressive aspects of the patient's mental functioning, long present . . . reemerge in forms that are clearer and easier to observe" does this not mean that the balance among the patient's defenses has shifted? Is this not what we mean by regression? Or shall we call such a shift "progressive" because it represents an undoing of *repression?* It seems clear that a more complex formula than the simple imputation of regression or progression is involved. If the regression remains confined to the therapeutic situation, it is a regression in the context of a progression. Insofar as it spills over into the outside world to any significant degree, it is regression proper rather than regression in the service of the ego.

All this aside, are the couch and frequent sessions necessary to bring about such a regression? I think not, but the issue is clearly one to be settled by experience and research rather than by debate. Furthermore, it is a matter of the individual patient and the particular patient–analyst dyad. Some people seen by some analysts five times a week and on the couch do not regress (however that is defined) in the analytic situation; some patients seen by some analysts once a week sitting up do regress.

That shifts in the balance among defenses are an integral part of a psychoanalytic process seems clear. They are an integral part of the pursuit of insight.

TRANSFERENCE: A DISTORTION?

Empirically the therapeutic situation is ineluctably an interactive one. The question is: What aspects of that interaction are desirable or possible to analyze? If the interaction is unwitting, there is less likelihood that it will be analyzed. It is important to remember that all interpretations, indeed all interventions, whether they relate to transference or extratransference material, whether contemporary or genetic, are interactions.

Of Oremland's belief that the therapist should be constrained in his activity in psychoanalytically oriented psychotherapy and psychoanalysis, I ask whether this view implies that the constraint will be an unanalyzed interaction. I am also concerned about Oremland's distinction between the psychotherapist as a person and the psychotherapist as a transference figure. I fear that some vestige of the view of transference as a distortion lurks in the distinction. Indeed, on a number of occasions Oremland refers to transference as a distortion in a way that suggests that he does not fully agree with my view that transference is *always* contributed to by both participants, however varying the proportion of inputs may seem to be. He writes, for example, "The patient's expectations of how the psychotherapist will react as contents are being revealed become the linchpin for distinguishing between the patient's experiencing of and the *actualities* of the interaction" (p. 44, italics added). I also take exception to his view in discussing errors and slips that "the regressive forces operating in the psychotherapeutic situation create a high likelihood that the error is the patient's and is transferentially significant" (see chapter 7). I believe his statement implies an underestimation of the therapist's involvement. I am not sure that Oremland agrees that the ubiquity of interaction is in principle incompatible with the idea of the transference ever being a "distortion" solely determined by the patient.

I have already distinguished between each participant "shaping" the other and each "reading" the other according to his own perspective. The latter principle is another way of stating the relationship between psychic and material reality. Everyone experiences the world as an integration of his or her intrapsychic schemata and external reality. We are ready to believe this of the patient but are prone to forget that it is equally true of the therapist. As I have already pointed out, there is no universal meaning to be imputed to an external event. What is called "distortion" in most discussions of how the patient experiences the therapist is a matter, rather, of how the patient selects from among possible readings. Another sense in which patient and analyst often "distort" their experience of each other is to regard that experience as an objectively correct, that is, an absolute reading. The issues here are complex; they are beginning to be explored in the literature on the constructivist model to which I referred earlier.

The principle of social–constructivism is so different from the classical psychoanalytic position that inevitably even those who espouse it will slip into the earlier paradigm from time to time. I have already referred to Oremland's rules about such things as announcements, as I myself have done. He corrects the error by disclaiming that such prescriptive guidelines are recommendations; he maintains that they are but illustrations of how certain situations can be handled. Still, these remarks have the flavor of recommendations, and in that sense they imply universal and possibly unanalyzed meanings, as Oremland well knows. Hoffman (1983, p. 406) has pointed out that the first half of my monograph on the analysis of transference (Gill, 1982) slips more than once into the old conceptual mold.

In his masterful monograph on technique, Fenichel (1941) wrote, "Everything is permissible, if only one knows why. Not external measures, but the management of resistance and transference is the criterion for estimating whether a procedure is analysis or not" (p. 24). *But to be analytic, it is not enough to "know why."* For the procedure to be analytic, one must also analyze the interactive meaning of the "everything." The therapist who knows may be psychoanalytically informed, but if he does not analyze what he knows, remaining alert to and trying to make explicit what is going on, the therapy is not analytic. This proviso should be understood to be true in the long run, not the short run. As I noted earlier, the therapist may decide that a particular interaction should not now be analyzed. Hoffman (personal communication) has laid special emphasis on this point. Furthermore, Hoffman and I (1988) have suggested that there may be an optimal alternating between phases of unwitting enactment in which the analyst falls into transference-countertransference patterns and witting phases of interpretation.

A one-sided emphasis on the analysis of transference without recognizing its position in the overall context of the therapy will itself have major interactive significance that probably would go unanalyzed. I failed to make this clear in my critique of Fenichel's monograph (Gill, 1980, 1981), in which I argued that he did not sufficiently emphasize the analysis of the transference.

Freud (1916-1917) considered the problem of suggestion to be central. Suggestion and interaction may not seem to be synonyms if suggestion is considered the psychoanalyst's input only. But from an interactive point of view, suggestion, like all else in the therapeutic situation, is the joint activity of patient and therapist. Freud (1933) thought he had disposed of suggestion in claiming that the analysis of the transference overcame it. He also wrote:

> . . . the uncertainty in all these matters is a constant instigation toward perfecting analysis and *in particular the transference*. Beginners in analysis especially are left in doubt in case of a failure whether they should blame the peculiarities of the case or their own clumsy handling of the procedure, but as I have said already, I do not think much can be achieved by efforts in this direction [pp. 154-155; italics added].

I tried to read "in particular the transference" to mean "in particular the analysis of the transference," but I cannot, because on the previous page Freud writes that what he means is "to intensify the transference"—that is interaction, not analysis. He is using the concept transference, as he often does, in the sense of the capacity for a relationship.

TERMINOLOGY AGAIN

I return to the difficult issue of terminology. I have noted that I do not like the term psychoanalytically oriented psychotherapy, for what Oremland describes under that name because the term implies psychotherapy in contrast to psychoanalysis. That both his "psychoanalytically oriented psychotherapy" and my (Gill, 1984b) "psychoanalytic technique" analyze interaction is far more important than that they differ in ambitiousness of goal and duration. And that they share the analysis of interaction in common with psychoanalysis proper is far more important than that they differ from the latter in the extrinsic factors of couch and frequency of sessions. Furthermore, as I said, the use of the term psychoanalytically oriented psychotherapy is so entrenched as a term for the continuum from exploratory psychotherapy to psychoanalysis that I do not see how it can be changed.

If the attempt to analyze the interaction is only partly or not at all successful, should the therapy be considered nonanalytic? I would argue against such a view. To me it seems reasonable to call analytic a therapy that analyzes the interaction as much as possible, although it may be an analytic failure if it turns out that little or no such analysis can be done. On the other hand, I would not call analytic a therapy in which some analysis of the interaction was done, but much not done that could have been done. In the latter case, analysis of the interaction was not pursued as a basic element in the technique. The emphasis should fall not on how much *is* done but on how much is done *of what could be done.* I realize that is a difficult judgment to make. Should the therapist's experience and ability be taken into account in making it? In other words, I suggest that much of what is now called psychoanalytic psychotherapy does not "deserve" to be called psychoanalytic; but I believe it probably will continue to be the main kind of psychotherapy done—a psychotherapy that falls somewhere along the continuum. I realize that to say "deserve" sounds moralistic. I mean it in the sense in which Freud wrote that if a therapy does not deal with transference and resistance, then whatever else it is, it is not analysis. To say that such and such work is good psychotherapy but not real analysis is a belittling cliché among many analysts. I hope that we are giving that expression new meaning. I should add, and I have said this earlier (Gill, 1984b), that an insistence on analyzing the transference where the patient is unable to tolerate it is a bad self-indulgence on the therapist's part.

With some hesitancy I would like to suggest a name for both

what Oremland calls "psychoanalytically oriented psychotherapy" and what I clumsily called "psychoanalytic technique." It is the revival of a term that Alexander and French (1946) used for their manipulative psychotherapy, which employed psychoanalytic understanding of psychodynamics. The term has so fallen into disuse that I believe it is available for a new purpose. I refer to the term "psychoanalytic therapy." I suggest that the term be used for a therapy in which the analysis of interaction is a primary goal, regardless of how ambitious or lengthy the therapy is, and in which the couch is not used and sessions are less frequent than in psychoanalysis proper. I am not sanguine about the prospects for my suggestion.

Oremland is opposed to this suggestion because it violates what for him is a major thesis of his study to which I referred earlier: the distinction between an emphasis on understanding and an emphasis on unexamined experiencing. He regards the analysis of interaction to be educative and broadly defined, and unanalyzed interaction to be therapeutic in a specific, although limited and limiting way; and my proposal invokes the term therapy for both. Of course, one might then ask why he is willing to characterize as psychoanalytically oriented *psychotherapy* a modality that analyzes interaction.

Furthermore, I cite this passage from Freud (1916–1917) in opposition to Oremland's view:

> This work of overcoming resistances is the essential function of analytic treatment; the patient has to accomplish it and the doctor makes this possible for him with the help of suggestion operating in an *educative* sense. For that reason psychoanalytic treatment has justly been described as a kind of *after-education* [p. 451].

Suggestion here clearly means using the transference without analyzing it; yet Freud relates this to education. Of course, Oremland may be using the concept of education in a different sense. Incidentally, in connection with my proposal for nomenclature, Freud's lecture in which the remark was made is called "Analytic Therapy" (*Die analytische Therapie*).

I believe that both Oremland and I imply that unanalyzed interaction is limited and limiting. This may well be a carryover from the classical analytic tradition according to which insight alone is mutative. We could be read to be implying that an effect based on interpersonal influence is not analytic. But there are many kinds of interpersonal influences in therapy, including new beneficent interactions that, it is hoped, will remain influential. We do mean to imply that if an interpersonal influence is properly analyzed, its effect becomes less tied to the specific patient–therapist interaction. And, of course, there are interactions that persist, no matter how carefully analyzed. The idea that psychoanalysis appropriately includes good interactions and not just education in insight has been gaining ground for some time, especially among interpersonalists and proponents of object relations theories. Even in classical analysis the analyst is now seen as much more a participant than only a "neutral" partner whose only appropriate contribution to the interaction is in a therapeutic alliance. In some quarters it is possible to speak of a "corrective emotional experience" without being misunderstood to be using the term in Alexander's manipulative sense (see Marohn and Wolf, 1990).

I believe that Oremland's dichotomy between the therapeutic and the after-educative will have to yield to a more complex interrelationship of the two. And I believe that the term "psychoanalytic therapy," as I define it, can encompass such complexity. It has the virtue of not including the term psychotherapy, which is so firmly fixed as being in opposition to psychoanalysis. But it does use the word therapy, and I fear that it will therefore be used as synonymous with the current meaning of "psychotherapy."

CONCLUSION

I close by reiterating the key issue on which Oremland and I agree, that is, the ubiquity of interaction and the distinction between unanalyzed interaction and analyzed interaction. I believe that the application of psychoanalytic technique can be expanded and that both briefer therapies and even psychoanalysis proper can be improved by assiduously following through on the implications of these propositions. The word assiduous is, of course, subject to a major misunderstanding. I mean assiduous in the sense of the therapist's acceptance of the principle, but the actual analysis of the interaction can be carried out only to the extent that the analyst is comfortable in doing so and judges such analysis to be assimilable by the patient—difficult criteria indeed. Even that way of putting it attributes too much awareness and control to the analyst. The interaction always has a number of simultaneous meanings, and the therapist cannot be aware of all of them at once, sometimes not even of the most important one. And sometimes he will feel completely at sea. A host of important questions about technique is implied in my use of the words "assimilable" and "comfortable." Further theoretical study and practical experience in the context of these ideas are sorely needed.

Oremland and I agree that the ideas in this book are encountering considerable resistance among analysts, because, some will argue, the proposed paradigm is less appropriate to the analytic situation than the old paradigm. We do not believe it is. Paradigms are notoriously difficult to change in any case, and in this instance there is an additional consideration. The application, as opposed to the mere acceptance, of these ideas requires a thorough-going acceptance of the reality and ubiquity of the interpersonally interactive nature of the therapeutic situation, or otherwise stated, the transference–countertransference dialectic, to use Oremland's phrase. It also requires a willingness to accept the fact that either we enter into an affective relationship with our patients or we defend ourselves against it. We have no other choice.

I believe a fitting conclusion, with a nod to the history of our field, is the summarizing statement from Szurek's little-known book *The Roots of Psychoanalysis and Psychotherapy* (1958). Although there is much to criticize in it from the viewpoint of this book, it is noteworthy for the spirit of moving all psychological therapy in a psychoanalytic direction:

> . . . in all therapeutic work, whatever the frequency, the duration, the form or severity of the patient's disorder, if the therapist is generally or is becoming more and more of a psychoanalyst with the particular patient, then his work cannot be other than psychoanalytic, or, perhaps more precisely, it will be moving steadily towards a classical psychoanalytic situation. And if we thus progressively learn and acquire more therapeutic skill and think more and more clearly about our experiences, then we may perhaps further refine "the gold of analysis"—or transmute it into an element even more rare on the earth—when we must work in the most

adverse of circumstances. We may then need less and less to alloy our procedures with some baser element like "the copper of suggestion" [pp. 120–121].

In present-day work, especially with the practical difficulties of acquiring a psychoanalytic practice, many clinical analysts do both psychotherapy and psychoanalysis. The psychotherapy is often heavily interactive, that is, without the analysis of interaction, because the therapist believes such analysis should be reserved for psychoanalysis. The result may be a deterioration in the analyst's work in analyzing the interaction in his analyses. Freud (1933) wrote that analysis is not like a pair of spectacles that one can put on and take off, that as a rule it possesses a man entirely or not at all (p. 153). Oremland's thoughtful study, in presenting a viewpoint that I see as aimed at making psychological therapy as psychoanalytic as possible, offers protection from these dangers. It should aid clinicians in retaining their analytic identities and their analytic orientation across the spectrum of their therapeutic work.

REFERENCES

Alexander, F. & French, T. (1946), *Psychoanalytic Therapy: Principles and Application.* New York: Ronald Press.
Arlow, J. (1975), Discussion of paper by M. Kanzer, "The therapeutic and working alliances." *Internat. J. Psycho-Anal. Psychother.,* 4:69–73.
Balint, M. (1965), *Primary Love and Psychoanalytic Technique.* New York: Liveright.
Bibring, E. (1954), Psychoanalysis and the dynamic psychotherapies. *J. Amer. Psychoanal. Assn.* 2:745–770.
Blum, H. (1983), The position and value of extra-transference interpretation. *J. Amer. Psychoanal. Assoc.,* 31:587–617.
Eissler, K. (1953), The effect of the structure of the ego on psychoanalytic technique. *J. Amer. Psychoanal. Assn.,* 1:104–143.
Fenichel, O. (1941), *Problems of Psychoanalytic Technique.* Albany: Psychoanalytic Quarterly.
Ferenczi, S. (1925), *Further Contributions to the Theory and Technique of Psychoanalysis.* London: Hogarth Press, 1950.
Freud, S. (1913), On beginning the treatment. *Standard Edition,* 12:121–144.
———— (1914), Repeating, remembering and working through (Further recommendations on the technique of psychoanalysis II). *Standard Edition,* 12:147–156, London: Hogarth, 1958.
———— (1916–1917), Introductory lectures on psychoanalysis. *Standard Edition* 15 & 16. London: Hogarth Press, 1963.

_____ (1919), Lines of advance in psycho-analytic therapy. *Standard Edition,* 17:158–271. London: Hogarth Press, 1955.

_____ (1933), New introductory lectures on psychoanalysis. *Standard Edition,* 22:5–182. London: Hogarth Press, 1964.

Gill, M. (1954), Psychoanalysis and exploratory psychotherapy. *J. Amer. Psychoanal. Assn.,* 2:771–797.

_____ (1980–81), The analysis of transference: A critique of Fenichel's *Problems of Psychoanalytic Technique. Internat. J. Psycho-Anal. Psychother.,* 8:45–66.

_____ (1982), Analysis of transference: Vol. 1, Theory and technique. *Psychological Issues,* 53. New York: International Universities Press.

_____ (1984a), Transference: A change in conception or only in emphasis? A response. *Psychoanal. Inq.,* 4:489–524.

_____ (1984b), Psychoanalysis and psychotherapy: A revision. *Internat. Rev. Psycho-Anal.* 1:161–180.

_____ (1988), Converting psychotherapy into psychoanalysis. *Contemp. Psychoanal.,* 24:262–274.

_____ (in press), Letter to the editor in response to Wallerstein's "Psychoanalysis and psychotherapy: An historical perspective." *Internat J. Psycho-Anal.*

Hoffman, I. Z. (1983), The patient as interpreter of the analyst's experience. *Contemp. Psychoanal.,* 19:389–422.

_____ (1991), Toward a social-constructivist view of the psychoanalytic situation. *Psychoanal. Dialog.,* 1:74–105.

_____ & Gill, M. (1988), Clinical reflections on a coding scheme. *Internat. J. Psycho-Anal.,* 69:55–64.

Kris, E. (1952), On inspiration. In: *Psychoanalytic Explorations in Art.* New York: International Universities Press, pp. 291–302, 1964.

Macalpine, I. (1950), The development of the transference. *Psychoanal. Quart.,* 19:501–539.

Mann, J. (1973), *Time-Limited Psychotherapy.* Cambridge, MA: Harvard University Press.

Marohn, R. C. & Wolf, E. S. ed. (1990), *Psychoanal. Inq.,* 10(3).

Racker, H. (1968), *Transference and Countertransference.* New York: International Universities Press.

Rangell, L. (1981), Psychoanalysis and dynamic psychotherapy: Similarities and differences twenty-five years later. *Psychoanal. Quart.,* 50:665–693.

Schafer, R. (1983), *The Analytic Attitude.* New York: Basic Books.

_____ (1985), Wild analysis, *J. Amer. Psychoanal. Assn.,* 33:275–299.

Stone, L. (1961), *The Psychoanalytic Situation.* New York: International Universities press.

Sullivan, H. S. (1953), *The Interpersonal Theory of Psychiatry.* New York: Norton.

Szurek, S. (1958), *The Roots of Psychoanalysis and Psychotherapy.* Springfield, IL: Charles Thomas.

Wallerstein, R. (1984), The analysis of transference: A matter of emphasis or of theory reformulation? *Psychoanal. Inq.,* 4:325–354.

_____ (1989), Psychoanalysis and psychotherapy: An historical perspective. *Internat. J. Psycho-Anal.,* 70:563–592.

_____ (in press), Response to Merton Gill's letter to editor, *Internat. J. Psycho-Anal.*

References

Abelin, E. (1971), The role of the father in the separation–individuation process. In: *Separation-Individuation,* ed. J. McDevitt & C. Settlage. New York: International Universities Press, pp. 229–252.

_____ (1977), Some further observations and comments on the earliest role of the father. *Internat. J. Psycho-Anal.,* 56:293–302.

Adler, M. H. (1970), Reporter, Panel on psychoanalysis and psychotherapy. *Internat. J. Psycho-Anal.,* 51:219–231.

Alexander, F. (1927), *Psychoanalysis of the Total Personality.* New York: Nervous and Mental Disease, 1930.

_____ (1946), Some quantitative aspects of psychoanalytic technique. *J. Amer. Psychoanal. Assn.,* 2:722–733.

_____ French, T. M. (1946), *Psychoanalytic Therapy.* New York: Ronald Press.

Arlow, J. (1975), Discussion of "The Therapeutic and Working Alliances." *Internat. J. Psychoanal. Psychother.* 4:69–73.

Balint, M. (1950), On the termination of analysis. *Internat. J. Psycho-Anal.,* 31:196–199.

_____ (1966), Sandor Ferenczi's technical experiments. In: *Psychoanalytic Techniques,* ed. B. B. Wolman. New York: Basic Books, pp. 147–167.

Bergmann, M. & Hartman, F., ed. (1976), *The Evolution of Psychoanalytic Technique.* New York: Basic Books.

Berliner, B. (1941), Short psychoanalytic psychotherapy: Its possibilities and its limitations. *Bull. Menn. Clin.* 5:204–213.

Bibring, E. (1937), Therapeutic results of psychoanalysis. *Internat. J. Psycho-Anal.,* 18:170–189.

_____ (1954), Psychoanalysis and the dynamic psychotherapies. *J. Amer. Psychoanal. Assn.,* 2:745–770.

Blum, H. (1983), The position and value of extratransference interpretation. *J.*

Amer. Psychoanal. Assn., 31:587–617.

Bollas, C. (1987), *The Shadow of the Object.* New York: Columbia University.

Bordin, E. S. (1974), *Research Strategies in Psychotherapy.* New York: Wiley.

Brenner, C. (1976), *Psychoanalytic Technique and Psychic Conflict.* New York: International Universities Press.

_____ (1979), Working alliance, therapeutic alliance, and transference. *J. Amer. Psychoanal. Assn.,* 27:137–158.

_____ (1982), *The Mind in Conflict.* New York: International Universities Press.

Breznitz, S. (1971), A critical note on secondary revision. *Internat. J. Psycho-Anal.,* 52:407–439.

Bridger, H. (1950), Criteria for the termination of analysis. *Internat. J. Psycho-Anal.,* 31:202–203.

Buxbaum, E. (1950), Technique of terminating analysis. *Internat. J. Psycho-Anal.,* 31:184–190.

Eissler, K. R. (1953), The effects of the structure of the ego on psychoanalytic technique. *J. Amer. Psychoanal. Assn.,* 2:567–594.

_____ (1958), Remarks on some variations in psychoanalytical technique. *Internat. J. Psycho-Anal.* 39:222–229.

English, O. S. (1965), Reporter, The essentials of psychotherapy as viewed by the psychoanalyst. *J. Amer. Psychoanal. Assn.,* 1:550–561.

Erikson, E. H. (1954), The dream specimen of psychoanalysis. *J. Amer. Psychoanal. Assn.,* 2:5–56.

_____ (1959), Identity and the life cycle. *Psychological Issues,* Monogr. No. 1. New York: International Universities Press.

Fairbairn, W. R. D. (1954), *An Object Relations Theory of the Personality.* New York: Basic Books.

Fenichel, O. (1924), From the terminal phase of an analysis. *The Collected Papers,* 1st Series. New York: Norton, 1953, pp. 27–31.

Ferenczi, S. (1912), Suggestion and psychoanalysis. In: *Further Contributions to the Theory and Technique of Psychoanalysis.* New York: Basic Books, 1952, pp. 55–68.

_____ (1913a), To whom does one relate one's dreams? In: *Further Contributions to the Theory and Technique of Psychoanalysis.* New York: Basic Books, 1952, p. 349.

_____ (1913b), Stages in the development of the sense of reality. In: *Sex and Psychoanalysis.* New York: Basic Books, 1950, pp. 213–239.

_____ (1919), On the technique of psychoanalysis. In: *Further Contributions to the Theory and Technique of Psychoanalysis.* New York: Basic Books, 1952, pp. 177–189.

_____ (1920), The further development of an active therapy in psychoanalysis. In: *Further Contributions to the Theory and Technique of Psychoanalysis.* New York: Basic Books, 1952, pp. 198–217.

_____ (1923), On forced phantasies. In: *Further Contributions to the Theory and Technique of Psychoanalysis.* New York: Basic Books, 1952, pp. 68–77.

_____ (1925), Contra-indications to the "active" psychoanalytical technique. In: *Further Contributions to the Theory and Technique of Psychoanalysis.* New York: Basic Books, 1952, pp. 217–230.

_____ (1933), Confusion of tongues between adults and the child. In: *The*

Problems and Methods of Psychoanalysis. New York: Basic Books, 1955, pp. 156–167.

Firestein, S. K. (1974), Termination of psychoanalysis of adults: a review of the literature. *J. Amer. Psychoanal. Assn., 22*:873–894.

Fisher, C. (1987), Reporter, Conversion of psychotherapy to psychoanalysis. *J. Amer. Psychoanal. Assn., 35*:713–726.

Freud, A. (1954), Problems of technique in adult analysis. *Bull. Phila. Assn. Psychoanal., 4*:44–69.

_____ (1965), *Normality and Pathology in Childhood.* New York: International Universities Press.

Freud, S. (1900), The interpretation of dreams. *Standard Edition,* 4 & 5. London: Hogarth Press, 1953.

_____ (1905a), On psychotherapy. *Standard Edition,* 7:257–268. London: Hogarth Press, 1953.

_____ (1905b), Fragment of an analysis of a case of hysteria. *Standard Edition,* 7:7–122. London: Hogarth Press, 1953.

_____ (1905c), Psychical (or mental) treatment. *Standard Edition,* 7:283–304. London: Hogarth Press, 1953.

_____ (1912), The dynamics of transference. *Standard Edition,* 12:97–108. London: Hogarth Press, 1958.

_____ (1913), On beginning the treatment. *Standard Edition,* 12:123–144. London: Hogarth Press, 1958.

_____ (1914a), Remembering, repeating and working-through. *Standard Edition,* 12:145–156. London: Hogarth Press, 1958.

_____ (1914b), On narcissism: An introduction. *Standard Edition,* 14:67–102. London: Hogarth Press, 1958.

_____ (1915), Observations on transference love. *Standard Edition,* 12:211–238. London: Hogarth Press, 1958.

_____ (1916–1917), Introductory lectures on psycho-analysis. *Standard Edition,* 15 & 16. London: Hogarth Press, 1963.

_____ (1917), Introductory lectures in psychoanalysis. *Standard Edition,* 15:448–463. London: Hogarth Press, 1963.

_____ (1919), Lines of advance in psycho-analytic therapy. *Standard Edition,* 17:158–271. London: Hogarth Press, 1955.

_____ (1925), Psycho-analysis and delinquency. *Collected Papers,* Vol. 5, ed. J. Strachey, London: Hogarth Press, 1952.

_____ (1926), The question of lay analysis, *Standard Edition,* 20:183–250. London: Hogarth Press, 1959.

_____ (1933), Dreams and occultism. *Standard Edition,* 22:31–57. London: Hogarth Press, 1964.

Fromm-Reichmann, F. (1950), *Principles of Intensive Psychotherapy.* Chicago: University of Chicago Press.

Gedo, J. (1979), *Beyond Interpretation.* New York: International Universities Press.

_____ (1981), Measure for measure: A response. *Psychoanal. Inq.,* 1:289–316.

Gill, M. (1954), Psychoanalysis and exploratory psychotherapy. *J. Amer. Psychoanal. Assn.,* 2:771–797.

_____ (1982), Analysis of transference. *Psychological Issues.,* Monogr. No. 53.

New York: International Universities Press.

_____ (1988), Converting psychotherapy into psychoanalysis. *Contemp. Psychoanal.* 24:262–274.

Glover, E. (1955), *The Technique of Psychoanalysis.* New York: International Universities Press.

Greenacre, P. (1954), The role of transference: Practical considerations in relation to psychoanalytic therapy. *J. Amer. Psychoanal. Assn.,* 2:671–684.

Greenson, R. R. (1965), The working alliance and working through. In: *Drives, Affects, Behavior,* Vol. 2, ed. M. Schur. New York: International Universities Press, pp. 277–314.

_____ (1967), *The Technique and Practice of Psychoanalysis.* New York: International Universities Press.

_____ (1970), The exceptional position of the dream in psychoanalytic practice. *Psychoanal. Quart.,* 39:519–549.

Guntrip, H. (1961), *Personality Structure and Human Interaction.* New York: International Universities Press.

Hartmann, H. (1939), *Ego Psychology and the Problem of Adaptation.* New York: International Universities Press, 1958.

_____ (1950), Psychoanalysis and developmental psychology. *The Psychoanalytic Study of the Child,* 5:7–17. New York: International Universities Press.

_____ Kris, E. & Loewenstein, R. M. (1946), Comments on the formation of psychic structure. *The Psychoanalytic Study of the Child,* 2:11–38. New York: International Universities Press.

Hoffer, W. (1950), Three psychological criteria for the termination of treatment. *Internat. J. Psycho-Anal.,* 31:194–195.

Hoffman, I. (1983), The patient as interpreter of the analyst's experience. *Contemp. Psychoanal.,* 19:389–422.

Holt, R. (1965), Beyond vitalism and mechanism: Freud's concept of psychic energy. In: *The Ego, Science and Psychoanalysis,* Vol. 11, ed. J. H. Masserman. New York: Grune & Stratton, 1967, pp. 1–44.

Horowitz, M., Marmor, C., Krupnick, J., Wilner, N., Kaltreider, N., Wallerstein, R. (1984), *Personality Styles and Brief Psychotherapy.* New York: Basic Books.

Jones, E. (1948), The criteria of success in treatment. In: *Papers on Psychoanalysis.* Boston: Beacon Press, 1961, pp. 379–383.

Joyce, J. (1986), *Ulysses,* New York: Random House.

Jung, C. G. (1963), *Memories, Dreams, Reflections.* New York: Pantheon.

_____ (1966), *Collected Works of C. G. Jung,* Vol. 15. Princeton, NJ: Princeton University Press.

Kernberg, O. (1967), Borderline personality organization. *J. Amer. Psychoanal. Assn.,* 15:641–685.

_____ (1968), The treatment of patients with borderline personality organization. *Internat. J. Psycho-Anal.,* 49:600–619.

Klein, G. (1973), *Psychoanalytic Theory.* New York: International Universities Press.

Klein, M. (1932), *The Psycho-Analysis of Children.* London: Hogarth Press, 1949.

_____ (1950), On the criteria for the termination of a psychoanalysis. *Internat. J. Psycho-Anal.,* 31:78–80.

_____ Isaacs, S. & Riviere, J. (1952), *Developments in Psycho-Analysis.* London: Hogarth Press.

Kohut, H. (1971), *The Analysis of the Self.* New York: International Universities Press.

_____ (1977), *The Restoration of the Self.* New York: International Universities Press.

_____ (1984), *How Does Analysis Cure?* ed. A. Goldberg & P. Stepansky. Chicago: University of Chicago Press.

_____ Seitz, P. (1963), Concepts and theories of psychoanalysis. In: *Concepts of Personality.* ed. S. Wepman & R. Heine. Chicago: Aldine, pp. 113–141.

Kris, E. (1951), Ego psychology and interpretation in psychoanalytic therapy. *Psychoanal. Quart.,* 20:15–30.

_____ (1952), *Psychoanalytic Explorations in Art.* New York: International Universities Press.

Lampl-DeGroot, J. (1975), Vicissitudes of narcissism and problems of civilization. *The Psychoanalytic Study of the Child,* 30:663–681. New Haven, CT: Yale University Press.

_____ (1976), Personal experience with psychoanalytic technique and theory during the last half-century. *The Psychoanalytic Study of the Child,* 31:283–296. New Haven, CT: Yale University Press.

Langs, R. (1978), *The Listening Process.* New York: Aronson.

_____ (1982), *Psychotherapy.* New York: Aronson.

Lietes, N. (1977), Transference interpretation only? *Internat. J. Psycho-Anal.* 58:275–287.

Loewald, H. W. (1951), Ego and reality. *Internat. J. Psycho-Anal.,* 10:195–212.

London, P. (1964), *Modes & Morals of Psychotherapy.* New York: Hemisphere, 1985.

Luborsky, L. (1988), *Who Will Benefit from Psychotherapy?* New York: Basic Books.

Macalpine, I. (1950), The development of the transference. *Psychoanal. Quart.,* 19:501–539.

Mahler, M. (1968), *On Human Symbiosis and the Vicissitudes of Individuation,* Vol. 1, New York: International Universities Press.

_____ Gosliner, B. J. (1955), On symbiotic child psychosis: Genetic, dynamic, and restitutive aspects. *The Psychoanalytic Study of the Child,* 10:195–212. New York: International Universities Press.

_____ Pine, F. & Bergman, A. (1975), *The Psychological Birth of the Human Infant.* New York: Basic Books.

McGovern, C. M. (1985), *Masters of Madness.* Hanover, NH: University Press of New England.

Menninger, K. (1936), *Theory of Psychoanalytic Technique.* New York: Science Editions, 1961.

Norman, H., Blacker, K. H., Oremland, J. D. & Barrett, W. G. (1976), The fate of the transference neurosis after termination of a satisfactory analysis. *J. Amer. Psychoanal. Assn.,* 24:471–498.

Nunberg, H. (1951), Transference and reality. *Internat. J. Psycho-Anal.,* 32:1–19.

Oremland, J. D. (1972), Transference cure and flight into health. *Internat. J. Psychoanal. Psychother.,* 1:61–75.

_____ (1973), A specific dream during the termination phase of successful psychoanalyses. *J. Amer. Psychoanal. Assn.,* 21:285–302.

_____ (1976), A curious resolution of a hysterical symptom. *Internat. Rev. Psycho-Anal.,* 3:473–477.

_____ (1978), "Perhaps" and "maybe" in dreams. *Internat. Rev. Psychoanal.,* 5:199–205.

_____ (1985), Kohut's reformulations of defense and resistance as applied in therapeutic psychoanalysis. In: *Progress in Self Psychology,* Vol. 1, ed. A. Goldberg. New York: Guilford Press, pp. 97–105.

_____ (1989), *Michelangelo's Sistine Ceiling.* New York: International Universities Press.

_____ Blacker, K. & Norman, H. (1975), Incompleteness in "successful" psychoanalysis. *J. Amer. Psychoanal. Assn.,* 23:819–844.

Peltz, M. (1987), Reporter, Panel on contributions to psychiatric nosology. *J. Amer. Psychoanal. Assn.,* 35:693–711.

Rangell, L. (1954a), Reporter, Psychoanalysis and dynamic psychotherapy—similarities and differences. *J. Amer. Psychoanal. Assn.,* 2:152–166.

_____ (1954b), Similarities and differences between psychoanalysis and dynamic psychotherapy. *J. Amer. Psychoanal. Assn.,* 2:734–745.

Reich, W. (1947), *The Mass Psychology of Fascism,* ed. M. Higgins & C. M. Raphael. New York: Farrar, Straus & Giroux, 1970.

Rieff, P. (1961), *Freud: The Mind of the Moralist.* New York: Anchor Books.

_____ (1968), *The Triumph of the Therapeutic.* New York: Harper & Row.

Rogers, C. (1942), *Counseling and Psychotherapy.* New York: Houghton Mifflin Co.

Roth, S. (1987), *Psychotherapy: The Art of Wooing Nature.* Northvale, NJ: Aronson.

Roustang, F. (1983), *Psychoanalysis Never Lets Go* (trans. N. Lukacher), Baltimore, MD: Johns Hopkins University Press.

Schafer, R. (1964), The clinical analysis of affects. *J. Amer. Psychoanal. Assn.,* 12:275–299.

_____ (1976), *A New Language for Psychoanalysis.* New Haven, CT: Yale University Press.

_____ (1985), Wild analysis, *J. Amer. Psychoanal. Assn.,* 33:275–299.

Schorske, C. E. (1981), *Fin-de-Siécle Vienna, Politics and Culture.* New York: Vintage Books.

Schwaber, E., ed. (1985), *The Transference in Psychotherapy.* New York: International Universities Press.

Shane, M. (1980), Countertransference and the developmental orientation and approach. *Psychoanal. Contemp. Thought,* 3:195–212.

Silber, A. (1973), Secondary revision, secondary elaboration and ego synthesis. *Internat. J. Psycho-Anal.,* 54:161–168.

Stone, L. (1954), The widening scope of indications for psychoanalysis. *J. Amer. Psychoanal. Assn.,* 2:567–594.

_____ (1961), *The Psychoanalytic Situation.* New York: International Universities Press.

_____ (1981), Some thoughts on the here-and-now in psychoanalytic technique and process. *Psychoanal. Quart.,* 50:709–733.

Strachey, J. (1934), The nature and therapeutic action of psychoanalysis. *Internat. J. Psychoanal.,* 50:275–292.

_____ (1962), The emergence of Freud's fundamental hypothesis. *Standard Edition,* 3:62–63. London: Hogarth Press, 1962.

Sullivan, H. S. (1953), *The Interpersonal Theory of Psychiatry.* New York: Norton.

Sulloway, F. J. (1979), *Freud, Biologist of the Mind.* New York: Basic Books.

Tyson, R. L. (1986), Countertransference evolution in theory and practice. *J. Amer. Psychoanal. Assn.,* 34:251–274.

Valenstein, A. F. (1974), Reporter, Panel on transference. *Internat. J. Psycho-Anal.,* 55:311–321.

_____ (1985), A developmental approach to transference: diagnostic and treatment considerations. In: *The Transference in Psychotherapy,* ed. E. A. Schwaber. New York: International Universities Press, 21–33.

Waldhorn, H. F. (1967), Reporter, The place of the dream in clinical psychoanalysis. In: *Monograph Series of the Kris Study Group of the New York Psychoanalytic Institute,* Monogr. 2. New York: International Universities Press.

Wallerstein, R. S. (1968), The psychotherapy research project of the Menninger Foundation: A semifinal view. *Res. Psychother.* 5:584–605.

_____ (1986), *Forty-two Lives in Treatment.* New York: Guilford Press.

Watson, J. D. (1968), *The Double Helix.* New York: Atheneum.

Weigert, E. (1952), Contribution to the problem of termination psychoanalyses. *Psychoanal. Quart.,* 21:465–480.

Wheelis, A. (1956), The vocational hazards of psycho-analysis. *Internat. J. Psycho-Anal.,* 30:69–74.

Winnicott, D. W. (1965), *The Maturational Process and the Facilitating Environment.* New York: International Universities Press.

_____ (1971), *Playing and Reality.* New York: Basic Books.

Zetzel, E. R. (1956), Current concepts of transference. *Internat. J. Psycho-Anal.,* 37:369–376.

_____ (1965), The theory of therapy in relation to a developmental model of the psychic apparatus. *Internat. J. Psycho-Anal.,* 46:39–52.

Index

173

JEROME D. OREMLAND, M.D. is Director, San Francisco Institute for Psychoanalytic Psychotherapy and Psychoanalysis; Clinical Professor of Psychiatry, University of California, San Francisco; and Chief of Psychiatry, San Francisco Children's Hospital and Medical Center. A faculty member of the San Francisco Psychoanalytic Institute, he is the author of *Michelangelo's Sistine Ceiling: A Psychoanalytic Study of Creativity* (1979).

MERTON M. GILL, M.D., is Emeritus Professor of Psychiatry, The University of Illinois Medical Center, Chicago, and Supervising Analyst at The Institute for Psychoanalysis, Chicago, and at the Chicago Center for Psychoanalysis.